Frequent Confession

Dom Benedict Baur, O.S.B.
Archabbot of St. Martin's Abbey, Bueron

Frequent Confession

Its place in the spiritual life

*Instructions and considerations for
the frequent reception of the
sacrament of Penance*

TRANSLATED BY PATRICK C. BARRY, S.J.

SCEPTER PUBLISHERS
Princeton, New Jersey

Originally published under the title *Die haüfige Beicht* by Verlag
Herder GmbH. & Co., Freiburg, in 1922. First English edition
published by St. Paul Publications, London, in 1959. Reprinted
in 1984 by Four Courts Press, Dublin.

Nihil obstat: Stephen J. Greene
                   Censor deputatus

Imprimi potest: Dermot, Archbishop of Dublin
                   February 29, 1980

This edition published in 1999 by Scepter Publishers
P.O. Box 1270, Princeton, NJ 08542
© Scepter Publishers

ISBN 1–889334–16–2

Typeset in ITC New Baskerville
Composition by Shoreline Graphics, Rockland, Maine
PRINTED IN THE UNITED STATES OF AMERICA

Contents

Introduction

"May you succeed in being, during this Holy Year, in a particularly willing and generous way, the ministers of the sacrament of Penance."[1] This was an appeal of the Holy Father in his 1983 *Letter to Priests* on the occasion of Holy Thursday. It follows the many references to the sacrament of Reconciliation in the documents issued in preparation for the Jubilee, as well as the urgent invitation made by him, several of his predecessors, and the Second Vatican Council to make priests more and more aware of their irreplaceable role in the ministry of sacramental forgiveness.

In this context, a new edition of Abbot Baur's *Frequent Confession* is certainly welcome. The book is considered by many people such a spiritual classic that it may seem unnecessary to write an introduction to this edition. However, the practice of frequent reception of the sacrament of Penance has been so neglected in recent years and so discouraged in certain places among the young and the not-so-young that it is imperative to emphasize that it is not true that frequent confession is an outmoded practice or a fad of the 1950s or an expression of post–World War II fervor, like the baby boom or young college graduates joining contemplative orders, which weren't fads either, but two concrete and visible expressions of a true Christian outlook on human life, something well worth pondering in these days of abortion and scarcity of religious vocations.

Responsible voices in the Church have spoken about the decline in the use of the sacrament of Penance. "You are surely as aware as I am," said Cardinal Oddi, "and even more aware because of your daily pastoral cares, that the number of confessions among the faithful has declined appreciably over the past decade and a half; while it is reported simultaneously that, despite the small number of confessions, almost everyone at Sunday Mass goes to Holy Communion. The implication of this phenomenon is obvious, and the opposite of healthy."[2]

Pope John Paul II himself made reference to this fact in his address to the American bishops during his visit to the United States in 1979. "In the face of a widespread phenomenon of our times, namely, that many of our people who are among the great numbers who receive Communion make little use of Confession, we must emphasize Christ's basic call to conversion. We must also stress that the personal encounter with the forgiving Jesus in the sacrament of Reconciliation is a divine means that keeps alive in our hearts and in our communities a consciousness of sin in its perennial and tragic reality, and that actually brings forth, by the action of Jesus and the power of his Spirit, fruits of conversion in justice and holiness of life. By this sacrament we are renewed in fervor, strengthened in our resolves, and buoyed by divine encouragement."[3]

In a famous passage of the 1943 encyclical on the Mystical Body of Christ, which Abbot Baur quotes and which Magisterial documents (particularly Pope John Paul II's) have repeatedly referred to in the last forty years, Pope Pius XII warned about "the opinions of those who assert that little importance should be given to the frequent confession of venial sins." He stated in very clear words that "to ensure more rapid progress day by day in the path of virtue, we will that the pious practice of frequent confession, which was introduced into the Church by the inspiration of the Holy Spirit, should be earnestly advocated." He cited some of the benefits to be derived from it: "Genuine self-knowledge is increased, Christian humility grows, bad habits are corrected, spiritual neglect and tepidity are resisted, the conscience is purified, the will strengthened, a salutary self-control is attained, and grace is increased in virtue of the sacrament itself."[4]

The Holy Father was echoing, with the firmness of the highest authority in the Church, the constant teaching of the masters of the interior life and, as Paul VI said in his first encyclical, "the interior life remains the great source of the Church's spirituality, her own proper way of receiving the illuminations of the Spirit of Christ, the fundamental and irreplaceable manifestation of her religious and social activity, an impregnable defense as well as an inexhaustible source of energy in her difficult contacts with the world."[5] Pope John Paul II has reminded us that "the ways on which the Council of this century has set the Church going, ways indicated by the late Pope Paul VI in his first encyclical, will continue to be for a long time the ways that all of us must follow."[6]

If we want to have interior life we must use the means, and frequent confession is one of the important means, very much related to others—humility, the struggle against venial sin and lukewarmness, self-discipline, openness to the sources of grace. In one of his homilies Monsignor Escrivá de Balaguer said: "The virtue of hope assures us that God governs us with his all powerful providence and that he gives us all the means we need.... And our conviction that we are nothing (it doesn't take a high degree of humility to recognize the truth that we are nothing but a row of zeros) will turn into irresistible strength, because Christ will be the one to the left of these zeros, converting them into an immeasurable figure! . . . To win the battles of the soul, the best strategy often is to bide one's time and apply the suitable remedy with patience and perseverance. . . . Our all-powerful and merciful Lord has granted us the precise means with which to conquer. As I have already mentioned, all we have to do is to use them, resolving to begin again and again at every moment, should it prove necessary. I would like to see you going to the holy sacrament of Penance, the sacrament of divine forgiveness, every week, and indeed whenever you need it, without giving in to scruples. Clothed in grace, we can cross mountains (cf. Ps 103: 10), and climb the hill of our Christian duty, without halting on the way." [7]

The concluding words of Pius XII in the paragraph of his encyclical quoted above were strong enough to settle the issue: "Let those, therefore, among the younger clergy who make light of or lessen esteem for frequent confession realize that what they are doing is alien to the Spirit of Christ and disastrous for the Mystical Body of our Savior." [8] But he found it necessary to discuss the subject again. In the 1947 encyclical on the liturgy he insisted: "Since the opinions expressed by some about frequent confession are completely foreign to the Spirit of Christ and his immaculate Spouse and are also most dangerous to the spiritual life, let us call to mind that with sorrow we wrote about this point in the encyclical on the Mystical Body. We urgently insist once more that what we expounded in very serious words be proposed by you for the serious consideration and dutiful obedience of your flock, especially to students for the priesthood and young clergy." [9] The mind of Pius XII on the matter was expressed again in his 1950 apostolic exhortation to the clergy, where he spoke of the importance of frequent confession for

priests and where he repeated the very same list of
benefits to be obtained from it that he had given seven
years earlier.[10]

Saints and popes before Pius XII had spoken about
the subject. To quote only one, who was both a pope
and a saint, Pius X in a 1910 encyclical wrote about the
means for spiritual growth that Jesus Christ so lavishly
communicates to his followers, "especially prayer, sacrifice and the sacraments. . . . False reformers, however,
despise these means. . . . In this respect the false reformers of former days are even surpassed by their
modern followers. These latter, wearing the mask of re-
ligiosity, discredit and despise these means of salvation,
especially the two sacraments which cleanse the penitent soul from sin and feed it with celestial food. Let
every faithful pastor, therefore, employ the utmost zeal
in seeing that the benefits of such great value be held in
the highest esteem. Let them never permit these two
works of divine love to grow cold in the hearts of
men." [11] Let us recall that to the pontificate of this
saintly pope belongs also the decree on the first reception of the sacraments of Penance and the Eucharist,[12]
which became of current interest in the seventies, as we
will see later.

What about more recent times? Has the Church of
the sixties, the seventies, and the eighties, the Church
of the twentieth-century council and the post-council,
the Church of Popes John and Paul and the two John
Pauls spoken concretely about frequent confession?
Has it not been in the post-conciliar years that the practice has been abandoned by so many people? The answer is that the Church has spoken often and clearly.

In the 1959 encyclical on the Curé of Ars, Pope
John XXIII spoke passionately about the work of St.
John Vianney as a confessor. His words show perfect

continuity with the teaching of his immediate predecessor on the matter and in the following he quoted the three references of Pius XII mentioned above. "Stirred by the example of the Curé of Ars, let all directors of souls see to it that they devote themselves generously and be equipped with the proper knowledge to this duty of such great importance, since it is here particularly that the divine mercy emerges victorious over human malice, and here that, freed from their sins, men are reconciled with God. These same men should also remember that 'with very serious words' our predecessor of happy memory, Pius XII, reproved the opinion of those who belittle the frequent use of the sacrament of Penance when it is a matter of venial sins. . . . And likewise we are completely confident that priests, before others, will faithfully obey the prescriptions of canon law which command them piously and at definite times to receive themselves the sacrament of Penance which is so necessary for the attainment of holiness. We are also confident that, as is fitting, they may have the highest esteem for and make use of those urgent exhortations which this same predecessor of ours more than once imparted 'with sorrowful soul.' " [13]

The Holy Father practiced what he preached. Pope John, who has sometimes been misrepresented, liked to write those retreat notes that have become after his death, together with many other things, an expression of his soul. In 1961, at age eighty, he wrote: "First of all: 'I confess to Almighty God.' During my whole life I have kept faithful to my practice of weekly confession. Several times during my life I have renewed my general confession." [14]

The Second Vatican Council used more than once the expression "frequent reception of the sacraments," [15] obviously referring to the only two sacraments that can be received often, namely, the Eucharist and the sacrament of Penance, and insisted, as we will see later, on the availability of priests to hear the confessions of the faithful, in the spirit of Christ the Shepherd, making themselves altogether and always ready whenever the sacrament is reasonably sought by the faithful. That is, using a happy expression of Pope John Paul II, "what the Spirit said to the Church through the Council of our time." [16]

Post-conciliar documents on the subject are abundant, directly from the popes and from different sacred congregations of the Holy See, always promulgated by the authority of the pope. The number of confessions has decreased in recent years. A priest here and there may have not encouraged, perhaps even discouraged, the practice of frequent confession. As a matter of fact, in a 1983 article on "How often should Catholics go to confession?" in a popular Catholic weekly, while several priests were quoted who stated the unchanging Magisterial teaching on the usefulness of frequent confession, nevertheless the author reported that "most priests interviewed for this article said that 'devotional confession,' the practice of going to confession weekly or monthly 'even in the absence of serious sin,' was not a good idea." [17] I don't know how many priests were interviewed—five? five hundred? It would be useful to know this. But evidently those who did not think frequent confession to be a good idea either were ignorant of or chose to disagree with the statements on the subject made by Pius XII, John XXIII, Paul VI, and John Paul II, all of which go back to the well-known teaching of *Mystici Corporis* quoted above. Interestingly enough—and sadly enough—the article was published less than two months after Pope John Paul II spoke to all the priests of the world about their "being, during this Holy Year, in a particularly willing and generous way, the ministers of the sacrament of Penance." [18]

We can certainly say that the teaching of the Church on frequent confession has not been any less frequent in the post-conciliar years. Shortly after the Council Pope Paul spoke about the need for penance in a long document that included the unchanging divine command of penance, the need for external expressions of penance, the unbreakable relationship between the internal spirit and the external acts of penance, and the specific recommendation that "it is very desirable for bishops and other pastors of souls to promote zealously more frequent use of the sacrament of Penance, and to promote extraordinary works of penance for the sake of expiation and impetration, especially during the Lenten Season." [19] It is interesting that Pope John Paul II has referred to this document in very explicit terms: "In the Church . . . there must be a lively-felt need for penance, both in its sacramental aspect, and in what concerns penance as a virtue. This second aspect was expressed by Paul VI in the apostolic constitution *Paenitemini.* One of the Church's tasks is to put into practice the teaching *Paenitemini* contains; this subject must be investigated more deeply by us in common reflection, and many more decisions must be made about it in a spirit of pastoral collegiality and with respect for the different traditions in this regard and the different circumstances of the lives of the people of today." [20]

A 1970 decree from the Congregation for Religious is quite straightforward: "Religious . . . should value highly the sacrament of Penance. . . . Religious should likewise hold in high regard the frequent use of this sacrament by which true knowledge of self is deepened, Christian humility is strengthened, spiritual direction is provided, and grace is increased. These and other wonderful effects not only contribute greatly to daily growth in virtue, but they are highly beneficial also to the common good of the community." So far the decree includes much about frequent confession that can be beneficial to all Christians, young and old, insights that teaching sisters could have shared with their students, instead of discouraging them—as has happened here and there, to the dismay of parents—from the practice. If the teachers could not see the parallel between this teaching and that of Pius XII in 1943, the decree itself refers to the encyclical of the Mystical Body. As for religious themselves, teaching sisters included, the Congregation for Religious is specific: "Therefore, religious, in their desire to strengthen in themselves union with God, should strive to receive the sacrament of Penance frequently, that is, twice a month. Superiors, on their part, should encourage this frequency and make it possible for the members to go to confession at least every two weeks and even oftener, if they wish to do so." [21]

The publication of the 1971 *Catechetical Directory* opened a new chapter on the subject. It is a painful chapter that deals explicitly with the question of First Confession and First Communion and, necessarily related to it, with the topic of frequent confession, as well as the reality and nature of sin and similar matters.

The *Catechetical Directory* declared that "keeping in mind the common and general practice which *per se* cannot be derogated without the approval of the Apostolic See, and also having heard the Conferences of Bishops, the Holy See judges it fitting that the practice now in force in the Church of putting Confession ahead of First Communion should be retained." [22] Some catechetical "experts" did not like it. The whole thing did not fit in with their outlook. Those who had criticized old legalisms became all of a sudden gold medalists in the gymnastics of the new legalism: Is this a binding norm? Does the *Directory* have the force of ecclesiastical law? Can children be compelled to go to confession? It is obvious that terms such as compulsion and regimentation should not enter into a positive and constructive preparation for the fruitful reception of the sacraments. The child will fruitfully and happily receive the sacrament of Penance before First Communion if he is encouraged and gently led to do so by parents, priests, and teachers who have the right and the duty to open to the child the sacramental channels of God's grace.[23] In this context the *Directory* wrote that "one should also keep in mind the usefulness of Confession, which retains its efficacy even when only venial sins are in question, and which gives an increase in grace and charity, increases the child's dispositions for receiving the Eucharist, and also helps to perfect the Christian life."[24]

Whatever experiments contrary to the practice of Confession ahead of First Communion were allowed, such permission was discontinued by a joint 1973 Declaration of the Sacred Congregations for the Sacraments and for the Clergy.[25]

In the 1975 letter sent on Pope Paul's behalf by his secretary of state, Cardinal Jean Villot, to the Italian National Liturgical Week, it is stated that "the Holy Father lays particular stress on the Confession of children, which must always precede First Communion, even if separated from it by a suitable interval." The same letter made a reference to the importance of frequent confession: "His Holiness also wishes to recall the attention of all—priests, religious and faithful—to the frequenting of this sacrament. There are people, unfortunately, who set little store by frequent confession: but this is not the mind of the Church. The new rite, too, recommends frequent confession, presenting it as a renewed commitment to increase the grace of Baptism, and as an opportunity and a stimulus to conform to Christ more closely and to become more and more docile to the voice of the Spirit." [26]

In spite of the above, a 1977 letter of the Sacred Congregation for the Sacraments and Divine Worship and the Sacred Congregation for the Clergy had to be issued because "discussion and doubt continue to exist in some parts of the Church and at some catechetical centers with regard to the Church's discipline of having children receive the sacrament of Penance prior to First Communion. A number of complaints and petitions on this point have reached the Apostolic See from bishops, priests, and parents." The letter clearly reconfirms the traditional discipline: "The need for safeguarding and fostering a worthy participation in the Eucharist has led the Church to establish it as a norm of its discipline and pastoral practice that Confession is to precede Holy Communion. In this way the right of the faithful—children as well as adults—to receive the sacrament of Reconciliation is likewise acknowledged." The official response to the question expressly submitted by an apostolic religious institute in this regard was given as an appendix. The letter also mentioned that "if each child is prudently and suitably brought at the time of First Communion to an interior conviction that the greatest purity is required for worthily receiving the Eucharist, that conviction will stay with him throughout life and will foster a much greater esteem for and more frequent use of the sacrament of Reconciliation." [27]

A few months before his death, Pope Paul addressed a group of American bishops during their *ad limina* visit: "Today we wish to speak to you, your fellow bishops, and brother priests in America about certain sacramental aspects of conversion, about certain dimensions of the sacrament of Penance or of Reconciliation." He spoke at length about the norms given by the Holy See in 1972 regarding general absolution in cases of grave necessity and asked for faithful observance of these norms. He spoke about First Confession: "Another important aspect of the penitential discipline of the Church is the practice of First Confession before First Communion. Our appeal here is that the norms of the Apostolic See be not emptied of their meaning by contrary practice. In this regard we repeat words we spoke last year to a group of bishops during their *ad limina* visit: 'The faithful would be rightly shocked that obvious abuses are tolerated by those who have received the charge of the episcopate, which stands for, since the earliest days of the Church, vigilance and unity.'" He spoke of frequent confession and he referred to the text of Pius XII: "We believe that conditions in the Church today—in your own dioceses and elsewhere—are ripe for a more diligent and frequent use of the sacrament of Penance. . . . Moreover, with regard to the practice of frequent confession, we ask you to recall to your priests and religious and laity—to all the faithful in search of holiness—the words of our predecessor Pius XII: 'Not without the inspiration of the Holy Spirit was this practice introduced into the Church.'" [28]

Later in the same year, addressing a group of Canadian bishops during another *ad limina* visit, Pope John Paul II touched on exactly the same points: "At this moment in the life of the Church there are two particular aspects of sacramental discipline that are worthy of the special attention of the universal Church, and I wish to mention them, in order to assist bishops everywhere.

... These two matters are the practice of first Confession before first Communion and the question of general absolution. ... With regard to children who have reached the age of reason, the Church is happy to guarantee the pastoral value of having them experience the sacramental expression of conversion before being initiated into the Eucharistic sharing of the Paschal Mystery. ... And once again let us assure all our people of the great benefits derived from frequent confession. I am indeed convinced of the words of my predecessor Pius XII: 'Not without the inspiration of the Holy Spirit was this practice introduced into the Church.' " [29] The last two addresses are mentioned in a footnote of Pope John Paul II's first encyclical, in reference to the lively-felt need for penance in the Church of today. [30]

As we would expect, the new *Code of Canon Law* confirms this discipline when it states that it is the responsibility of parents and those who take the place of parents, as well as of pastors, to see to it that children who have reached the age of reason are given adequate preparation to receive Holy Communion as early as possible, preceded by sacramental confession. [31]

More recently still, as the first group of American bishops made their *ad limina* visit in the Holy Year of the Redemption, the Pope told them: "I would ask once again for your zealous pastoral and collegial solicitude to ensure that these norms [the Holy Father was referring to the norms of general absolution], as well as the norms regulating the First Confession of children, are understood and properly applied. The treasures of God's love in the sacrament of Penance are so great that children too must be initiated into them. The patient effort of parents, teachers, and priests needed to prepare children for this sacrament are of great value for the whole Church." [32]

We have mentioned together, without trying to be exhaustive, a number of texts that made reference to the benefits of frequent confession, while confirming over and over again the practice of First Confession before First Communion. During the same years, the subject of the frequent reception of the sacrament of Penance was mentioned in a broader context. The 1972 norms from the Sacred Congregation for the Doctrine of the Faith stated that "priests should be careful not to discourage the faithful from frequent or devotional confession. On the contrary, let them draw attention to its fruitfulness for Christian living (cf. *Mystici Corporis*) and always display readiness to hear such a confession whenever a reasonable request is made by the faithful. It must be absolutely prevented that individual confession should be reserved for serious sins only, for this would deprive the faithful of the great benefit of confession and would injure the good name of those who approach the sacrament singly." [33]

The 1973 Rite of Penance includes the recommendation of frequent confession: "Frequent and careful celebration of this sacrament is also very useful as a remedy for venial sins. This is not a mere ritual repetition or psychological exercise, but a serious striving to perfect the grace of Baptism so that, as we bear in our body the death of Jesus Christ, his life may be seen in us ever more clearly." [34]

During the 1975 Holy Year, Pope Paul VI wrote his Apostolic Exhortation on Christian Joy. Together with the many other reasons for joy, there is always for the sinner the joy of the prodigal son who returns home: "And because . . . all of us in fact remain to some extent sinners, we must today cease to harden our hearts, in order to listen to the voice of the Lord and accept the offer of the great pardon. . . . What burden is more crushing than that of sin? What distress more lonely than that of the prodigal son, described by the Evangelist St. Luke? On the other hand, what meeting is more overwhelming than that of the Father, patient and merciful, and the son returned to life? . . . And who is without sin, apart from Christ and his Immaculate Mother? Thus, by its invitation to return to the Father by repentance, the Holy Year—a promise of jubilation for all the people—is also a call to rediscover the meaning and practice of the sacrament of Reconciliation. Following the line of the best spiritual tradition, we remind the faithful and their pastors that the confession of grave sins is necessary and that frequent confession remains a privileged source of holiness, peace and joy." [35]

The popes have taught unequivocally. It is up to all of us to ponder this teaching, to put it into practice in our personal lives, and to bring it to others. Abbot Baur's book is good and solid reading to make frequent confession a source of spiritual progress, a means to walk over and over again the path of the prodigal son. Abbot Baur refers to this parable in part II, chapter 6. Pope John Paul II made a moving exegesis of the parable in his second encyclical,[36] as spiritual writers have done over the centuries. Monsignor Escrivá de Balaguer has written: "Remember the parable which Jesus told to help us understand the love of the Father who is in heaven: the parable of the prodigal son? 'But while he was still a long way off, his father saw him and took pity on him; running up he threw his arms around his neck and kissed him' (Lk 15: 20). That's what the sacred text says: he covered him with kisses. Can you put it more humanly than that? Can you describe more graphically the paternal love of God for men? . . . Human life is in some way a constant returning to our Father's house.

We return through contrition, through the conversion of heart which means a desire to change, a firm decision to improve our life and which, therefore, is expressed in sacrifice and self-giving. We return to our Father's house by means of the sacrament of pardon in which, by confessing our sins, we put on Jesus Christ again and become his brothers, members of God's family."[37]

The three synoptic Gospels describe the cure of a paralytic at Caphernaum (Mt 9: 1–8; Mk 2: 1–12; Lk 5: 17–26). "On one of those days, as he was teaching, there were Pharisees and teachers of the law sitting by, who had come from every village of Galilee and Judea and from Jerusalem" (Lk 5: 17).

We can picture them on their way to Caphernaum, singly or in groups, many of them curious, some of them talking about the prophet from Nazareth, what they have heard about his amazing teachings or his miracles. "And the power of the Lord was with him to heal" (Lk 5: 17).

We don't know what our Lord was talking about that day. All of a sudden his speech is interrupted. "And behold, men were bringing on a bed a man who was paralyzed, and they sought to bring him in and lay him before Jesus" (Lk 5: 18). We admire the friendship of these men who have brought the paralytic, their desire to have him touched by Christ's mercy, their trust in the Master. But even more we admire their determination and their daring. "But finding no way to bring him in, because of the crowd, they went up on the roof and let him down with his bed through the tiles into the midst before Jesus" (Lk 5: 19).

Our Lord seems to forget about everyone else for a moment. "And when he saw their faith he said, 'Man, your sins are forgiven you' " (Lk 5: 20).

We can watch the Gospel scene from whatever angle we want. It is good to learn to play a part in the scenes, to remember that in every one of those happenings we are there, that our Lord gives his teaching and performs the miracles not only for the sake of those who were physically present, but for every one of us. "Make it a habit to mingle with the characters who appear in the New Testament," Monsignor Escrivá wrote. "Capture the flavor of those moving scenes where the Master performs works that are both divine and human, and tells us, with human and divine touches, the wonderful story of his pardon for us and his enduring love for his children. Those foretastes of Heaven are renewed today, for the Gospel is always true: we can feel, we can sense, we can even say we touch God's protection with our own hands." [38]

We can, for the time being, be part of the crowd at the house of Caphernaum, each one of us one of those who have come from every village of Galilee and Judea and from Jerusalem. There is embarrassment and consternation around us. "And the scribes and the Pharisees began to question, saying, 'Who is this that speaks blasphemies? Who can forgive sins but God only?' " (Lk 5: 21).

There is no need for them to speak up. "When Jesus perceived their questioning, he answered them, 'Why do you question in your hearts? Which is easier to say, your sins are forgiven you, or to say, rise and walk?' " (Lk 5: 22–23). Both, of course, are impossible to a man. Only God can forgive sins; in this the Pharisees were right. And only God can cure a paralytic. " 'But that you may know that the Son of Man has authority on earth to forgive sin'—he said to the man who was paralyzed— 'I say to you, rise, take up your bed and go home.' And immediately he rose before them, and took up that on which he lay, and went home, glorying God" (Lk 5: 24–25).

We can relive once more the Gospel scene, taking the place of the paralytic, letting the eyes of Christ rest on us with tenderness, seeing our hearts. It happens every time we go to confession. "That you may know that the Son of Man has authority on earth to forgive sins. . . ." The risen Christ, he who has authority to forgive sins, told the Apostles: "Whose sins you shall forgive, they are forgiven them" (Jn 20: 23). The Church has authoritatively interpreted these words of Christ. "Our Lord instituted the sacrament of Penance notably on the occasion when, after his Resurrection, he breathed upon his disciples, saying, 'Receive the Holy Spirit, whose sins you shall forgive, they are forgiven them; and whose sins you shall retain, they are retained' (Jn 20: 22–23). The universal agreement of the Fathers has always understood that by such a striking action and by such clear words the power of remitting and retaining sins and of reconciling the faithful who have fallen after Baptism was communicated to the Apostles and their legitimate successors." [39]

It happened in the Upper Room, where on Holy Thursday Christ had instituted the Eucharist and, inseparably linked to it, the ministerial priesthood, where he had given the new commandment of charity and prayed to the Father for unity, promised the Holy Spirit, and spoke of friendship. "No longer do I call you servants . . . but I have called you friends" (Jn 15: 15). As John Paul II has said, "It was precisely in the Upper Room that those words were spoken, in the immediate context of the Eucharist and of the ministerial priesthood. Christ made known to the Apostles and to all those who inherit from them the ordained priesthood that in this vocation and for this ministry they must become *his friends*—they must become the *friends of that mystery* that he came to accomplish." [40]

It was fittingly in the same setting that the sacrament of Penance was instituted, so that we may keep alive the inseparable bond between the Eucharist and the call to conversion, so that the sacrament of Confession be understood as a purification in view of the Eucharist, as well as a testimony of faith in the dynamic sanctity of the Church and a need of the Church which is wounded in its totality by every sin.[41]

"How eloquent is the fact," the Pope comments, "that Christ, after his Resurrection, once more entered that Upper Room in which on Holy Thursday he had left the Apostles, together with the Eucharist, the sacrament of the ministerial priesthood, and that he then said to them: 'Receive the Holy Spirit; whose sins you shall forgive, they are forgiven them; and whose sins you shall retain, they are retained' (Jn 20: 22–23). Just as he had previously given them the power to celebrate the Eucharist, or to renew in a sacramental manner his own paschal Sacrifice, so on this second occasion he gave them the power to forgive sins. During this Jubilee Year, when you meditate on how your ministerial priesthood has been inscribed in the mystery of Christ's Redemption, you should have this constantly before your eyes!"[42]

It was in that same Upper Room that fifty days later the same Spirit came in the full force of Pentecost and the Church was born. It is good that we identify with the paralytic at Caphernaum when we go to confession, making use of our individual right to that encounter with the merciful Christ, and letting Christ exercise his right as our Redeemer, as the Holy Father reminded us in his first encyclical, referring specifically to the cure of the paralytic and the forgiveness of the adulterous woman: "In faithfully observing the centuries-old practice of the sacrament of Penance—the practice of individual confession with a personal act of sorrow and the intention to amend and make satisfaction—the Church is therefore defending the human soul's individual right to a more personal encounter with the crucified forgiving Christ, with Christ saying through the minister of the sacrament of Reconciliation: 'Your sins are forgiven' (Mk 2: 5); 'Go and do not sin again' (Jn 8: 11). As is evident, this is also a right on Christ's part with regard to every human being redeemed by him: his right to meet each one of us in that key moment of conversion and forgiveness." [43]

Every time we receive the sacrament of Reconciliation we can have in front of our eyes the Gospel scene at Caphernaum and take the place of the paralytic. But it is also necessary for many in the Church today to re-live that scene taking yet another part, that of the friends of the paralytic. They brought him in, met obstacles, and overcame them. They didn't say: "Sorry, we have tried, but there is a big crowd and there is no room. . . . The Master is busy, we do not want to bother him. . . . You wouldn't want us to bother him. . . . Let us take you home. . . . Perhaps another day. . . ."

Precisely because confession has been neglected and frequency of confession even discouraged—the popes have said so, as we saw in some of the quotations above —there is a need for an intense apostolate of the confessional, whose duty falls on everyone. There is a duty to encourage others, gently of course, to bring them to the forgiving Christ as the friends of the paralytic brought him.

The apostolate of the confessional is, above all, the duty of priests. The Second Vatican Council said: "[Priests] are united with the intention and love of Christ when they administer the sacraments. This is true in a special way when in the performance of their duty in the sacrament of Penance they show themselves altogether and always ready whenever the sacrament is reasonably sought by the faithful."[44] It does not seem that the bishops of the Council were one bit worried about priests being too busy to spend their time hearing confessions. They thought that priests should make themselves available to administer the sacrament of Penance whenever any of the faithful reasonably seeks it, be it Saturday afternoon or any other afternoon, morning, or evening, since confession should, within reason, be available at any time of the day.

In another Council document, addressed primarily to bishops, it is said that "[pastors] should labor without stint that the faithful be nourished with spiritual food through the devout and frequent reception of the sacraments and through intelligent participation in the Liturgy. Pastors should also be mindful of how much the sacrament of Penance contributes to developing the Christian life, and therefore, should always make themselves available to hear the confessions of the faithful."[45]

Pope Paul VI taught perseveringly the same idea. In 1975 the Vatican secretary of state wrote that "His Holiness directs a word especially to priests so that they may love this sacred ministry, prepare their faithful in its catechesis, and be always ready to hear their Confessions. The new rite offers many possibilities to enhance the sacrament, especially in the context of a celebration of the word of God. But nothing will be so important as the willingness of pastors of souls to maintain regular attendance at the confessional."[46]

The Holy Father himself put it, a few years later, in even stronger terms: "We ask you, the bishops, to help your priests to have an even greater appreciation of this splendid ministry of theirs as confessors. The experience of centuries confirms the importance of this ministry. And if priests deeply understand how closely they collaborate, through the sacrament of Penance, with the Savior in the work of conversion, they will give themselves with ever greater zeal to this ministry. More confessors will readily be available to the faithful." In case there was any doubt, in case some priests might think that other activities already occupied their time, the Pope continued: "Other works, for lack of time, may have to be postponed, but not the confessional." Priests have a great tradition to follow and the Holy Father concluded by saying: "The example of St. John Vianney is not outmoded. The exhortation of Pope John in his encyclical *Sacerdotii nostri primordia* is still extremely relevant." [47]

After quoting the above, Pope John Paul II told the Canadian bishops: "In the name of the Lord Jesus, let us give assurance, in union with the whole Church, to all our priests of the great supernatural effectiveness of a persevering ministry exercised through auricular confession, in fidelity to the command of the Lord and the teaching of his Church." [48]

On the occasion of Holy Thursday, at the beginning of the Holy Year of Redemption, the Pope said: "My dear brothers in the priesthood of Christ! During the Jubilee Year may you succeed in being in a special way the teachers of God's truth about forgiveness and remission, as this truth is constantly proclaimed by the Church. Present this truth in all its spiritual richness. Seek the ways to impress it upon the minds and consciences of the men and women of our time." [49]

As the American bishops began their *ad limina* visits in the Holy Year, John Paul II reiterated his wish that the sacrament of Penance be given special priority: "We are truly called to proclaim the reconciliation of humanity with God. . . . Proclaiming reconciliation means reviving a sense of sin among our people. . . . Proclaiming reconciliation means insisting on the greatness of God's pardon and on his compassionate love. . . . To proclaim reconciliation means in a particular way promoting the sacrament of Penance."[50]

Then the Holy Father, making frequent references to the address of Paul VI to the New York bishops five years before, asked them to make sure that the norms for general absolution and for the first confession of children "are understood and properly applied," and called for renewed catechetical efforts, "frequent penitential celebrations including the individual confession and absolution of sins," and greater availability of confessors.

In 1983 the Holy Father came down to practical details: "The availability of confessors, emphasized and publicized in different ways, such as church bulletins, can give a great impetus to the faithful to go to confession, since God's grace has already awakened a desire or need for the sacrament in the hearts of many."[51]

Every priest can make an easy calculation: so many thousands of people in the parish, so many priests available for confessions for so many hours per week. Is it enough? Granted that some of the parishioners may go elsewhere, but the relative number of those will almost always be small. Granted that a few may seek Confession at any time "by appointment." However, as the late Cardinal Medeiros pointed out in a Lenten pastoral letter, "it is pastorally important for us to make ourselves available in the confessional on a regular basis at a designated time which is convenient for those seeking the sacrament. It is never sufficient for us merely to announce that we are available by appointment. Most parishioners are hesitant to take that kind of initiative and look for us. Even if few take advantage of the opportunity, our continuing presence in the confessional speaks eloquently of our own faith and conviction regarding the centrality of this priestly ministry to others. It is a witness to Christ's availability and readiness to forgive. He came to save sinners at any time and at all times!" [52]

Catechesis on confession and availability for confessions were constant themes of the Holy Year and must continue after the Holy Year. Many different aspects of the sacrament of Penance have to be emphasized, rediscovered, and, if need be, discovered for the first time. It may be necessary to return to basics, such as explaining with clarity, for example, what is meant by "integrity of confession," what is meant by "kind, number, and circumstances that change the nature of the sin," to spell out without ambiguity the criterion given in so many of the post-conciliar documents and in the new *Code of Canon Law*[53] that no one who is conscious of having committed mortal sin, even if he believes himself to be contrite, should approach the Holy Eucharist without first making a sacramental confession, except in rather unusual circumstances. All this will require an explanation, with concrete examples if need be, about the two kinds of actual sin: mortal sin and venial sin, about formation of conscience, and so on.

We may have to speak again about the advantages of frequent confession, since the sacrament of Penance is both a means of conversion and a means of spiritual progress. We may have to speak about the benefits of having a fixed confessor and the smooth transition from frequent confession to spiritual direction.

We may have to speak about the value of the confessions of children and repeat the norms regarding the First Confession. The experience of Monsignor Escrivá,

FREQUENT CONFESSION

who loved the apostolate of the confessional and helped many souls to love it, was heard a few months before his death: "I have upon my conscience—and I say it with pride—having dedicated many, many thousands of hours to hearing children's Confessions in the poor districts of Madrid. I would have liked to have gone to hear Confessions in all the saddest and most abandoned slums of the whole world. They used to come to me with runny noses. First you had to clean their noses, before cleaning their poor souls a little. Bring children to God, before the devil gets them. Believe me, you will do them a lot of good. I speak from experience, from the experience of thousands of souls, and from my own experience." [54]

The apostolate of the confessional is also the duty of others: parents, teachers, friends. It can never involve pushing or forcing, because any true apostolate is incompatible with that, and also because the reception of the sacrament of Penance requires freedom. It is rather a question of example and encouragement, backed by prayer and the conviction that those who exercise this apostolate and any other apostolate are only instruments of God's grace.

Any time is a fitting time for the apostolate of bringing others to the forgiving Christ as the friends of the paralytic brought him. The Lenten season offers a special opportunity every year. Every Jubilee by its very nature brings another such opportunity, as Pope Paul reminded us in 1975.[55] In all the documents written in preparation for the Jubilee of the Redemption, the Holy Father insisted on the role of confession. In his address of December 23, 1982, he said: "The approaching Jubilee is intended to make people more aware of the celebration of the Redemption. . . . Its specific purpose is to call to a more profound consideration of the event of Redemption and its concrete application in the sacrament of Penance."[56]

It is not enough to consider the objective reality of Redemption. Each one of us has to "touch" Redemption or, perhaps better, Redemption has to "touch" each one of us. In the same address, Pope John Paul II continues: "The sacrament of Penance is the sacrament of reconciliation with God, the encounter of the misery of man with the mercy of God personified in Christ the Redeemer and in the power of the Church. Confession is a practical exercise of faith in the event of Redemption. The sacrament of Confession is therefore reproposed, through the Jubilee, as a testimony of faith in the dynamic sanctity of the Church. . . . It is reproposed as a need of the ecclesial community. . . . It is reproposed as a purification in view of the Eucharist."[57]

The Bull of Indiction of the Jubilee contained several clear references to the sacrament of Penance. "In order to return to the state of grace, in ordinary circumstances it is not sufficient internally to acknowledge one's guilt and to make external reparation for it. Christ the Redeemer . . . established that the salvation of the individual should come about within the Church and through the ministry of the Church (cf. *Ordo paenitentiae*, n. 46). . . . It is true that the ways of the Lord are inscrutable . . . but the 'way' that Christ made known to us is through the Church which, by means of the sacrament, or at least the 'desire' for it, reestablishes a new personal contact between the sinner and the Redeemer."[58]

The Holy Father recalled that "it is a demand of the very Mystery of Redemption that the ministry of reconciliation entrusted by God to the Shepherds of the Church (cf. 2 Cor 5: 18) should find its natural accomplishment in the sacrament of Penance"[59] and stated that "certainly the Fathers of the Synod will, together with me, devote particular attention to the irreplaceable role of the sacrament of Penance in the saving mission of the Church."[60]

Finally, in the portion of the document devoted to the "gift of the indulgence, proper to and characteristic of the Jubilee Year," the Pope reminded us that "the indulgence is inseparable from the power and sacrament of Penance"[61] and that "individual and complete sacramental confession, wherein takes place the encounter between man's misery and God's mercy," is one of the conditions for gaining a plenary indulgence.[62]

In his letter of January 25, 1983, to all the bishops of the world on the occasion of presentation of the working paper for the Synod, "since one of the main purposes of the Holy Year of the Redemption is to ensure that the renewing power of the Church's sacramental life be lived especially intensely, and indeed, if necessary, to ensure that this power be rediscovered," the Holy Father said: "All of you, dear Brothers in the Episcopate, will have to make a special effort to present and put into practice an ever more appropriate strategy regarding the sacraments. This will include devoting very special attention to the sacrament of Penance." He then encouraged the use of all pastoral means available, including "the presence of priests in the main churches who will ensure that at any hour of the day individuals can receive the sacrament of Penance."[63]

It is not possible to collect here all the references to the sacrament of Penance made by Pope John Paul II throughout the Jubilee of the Redemption, including the series of nine General Audience talks given at the end of the Holy Year (February 22 to April 18, 1984),[64] which constitute a complete catechesis on the sacrament. Nor is it possible to discuss here the interventions of the participants in the 1983 Synod of Bishops.

If the Year of the Redemption was meant "to leave a special imprint on the Church's whole life," [65] we cannot underestimate the part to be played by the sacrament of Penance. Perhaps we can venture to say that our fidelity to the graces of the Jubilee will be measured to a great extent by our commitment to exercise for and with Christ a persevering apostolate of the confessional.

And yet this cannot be an apostolate that springs from norms and regulations but, much more radically, from a deeper awareness on the part of the People of God, both priests and laity, of the meaning and practice of the sacrament. It needs to be a grass-roots apostolate. Perhaps this is one of the areas where the movement has to be "from below," [66] beginning with the individual parish and the individual Catholic.

Mary is, Pope John Paul II has reminded us, "the Mother in whom we trust" and "we who form today's generation of disciples of Christ all wish to unite ourselves with her in a special way. . . . We do so at the urging of the deep need of faith, hope and charity."[67] We can certainly entrust to her this urgently needed apostolate of the confessional. As the Holy Father said in the first year of his pontificate, "she is the refuge of sinners. . . . If we are oppressed by awareness of sin, we instinctively seek him who has the power to forgive sins (cf. Lk 5: 24), and we seek him through Mary, whose sanctuaries are places of conversion, penance, and reconciliation with God. She awakens in us the hope of mending our ways and persevering in good, even if that may sometimes seem humanly impossible. She enables us to overcome the multiple "structures of sin" in which our personal, family, and social life is wrapped.

She enables us to obtain the grace of true liberation, with that freedom with which Christ liberated every man." [68]

S. M. Ferigle
Boston, June 25, 1984

---

[1] John Paul II, *Letter to Priests*, March 27, 1983, no. 3.

[2] Cardinal Silvio Oddi, "The Priesthood of Today and Tomorrow," address at St. Charles Borromeo Seminary in Philadelphia for the 150th anniversary of its foundation (New Rochelle, N.Y., 1983) p. 20.

[3] John Paul II, address to American bishops, October 5, 1979, no. 9.

[4] Pius XII, encyclical *Mystici Corporis*, June 29, 1943 (NCWC edition), no. 88.

[5] Paul VI, encyclical *Ecclesiam Suam*, August 6, 1964, n. 38.

[6] John Paul II, encyclical *Redemptor hominis*, March 4, 1979, no. 7.

[7] Josemaría Escrivá, *Friends of God* (Dublin, London, New York, 1981), nos. 218–219. A number of references to the teachings of the founder of Opus Dei on the sacrament of Penance are given in the article "The Pardoning Sacrament," published in Bulletin No. 5 on the life of Monsignor Escrivá. Copies of this and other issues can be obtained in the United States from Bulletin on the Life of Msgr. Escrivá, 330 Riverside Dr., New York, N.Y. 10025, and, in Ireland, from Harvieston, Cunningham Road, Dalkey, County Dublin.

[8] *Mystici Corporis*, no. 88.

[9] Pius XII, encyclical *Mediator Dei*, November 20, 1947 (NCWC edition), no. 177.

[10] Pius XII, apostolic exhortation *Menti nostrae*, September 23, 1950.

[11] Pius X, encyclical *Editae saepe*, May 26, 1910.

[12] Decree *Quam singulari*, August 8, 1910.

[13] John XXIII, encyclical *Sacerdotii nostri primordia*, August 1, 1959 (NCWC edition), no. 56.

[14] *Journal of a Soul* (New York, 1965), pp. 304–305.

[15] Decree on the Pastoral Office of Bishops, *Christus Dominus*, no. 30; see also Constitution on the Sacred Liturgy, *Sacrosanctum concilium*, no. 59.

[16] *Redemptor hominis*, no. 3.

[17] Maggie Grevatt, "Confession: 'How often should I go to confession?' Priests debate," in *Catholic Twin Circle*, May 15, 1983.

[18] John Paul II, *Letter to Priests* (1983), no. 3.

[19] Paul VI, apostolic constitution *Paenitemini*, February 17, 1966.

[20] *Redemptor hominis*, no. 20.

[21] Sacred Congregation for Religious, Decree on Confessions for Religious, December 8, 1970.

[22] Sacred Congregation for the Clergy, *General Catechetical Directory*, April 11, 1971, addendum, no. 5.

[23] See the authoritative article by Cardinal John Wright, "The New Catechetical Directory and Initiation to the Sacrament of Penance and the Eucharist," *L'Osservatore Romano*, English ed., October 7, 1971.

[24] *General Catechetical Directory*, addendum, no. 5.

[25] Sacred Congregation for the Discipline of the Sacraments and Sacred Congregation for the Clergy, Declaration *Sanctus Pontifex*, May 24, 1973.

[26] Letter of the Secretary of State, Cardinal Jean Villot, to the 26th Italian National Liturgical Week, which opened in Florence on August 25, 1975.

[27] Sacred Congregation for the Sacraments and Divine Worship and Sacred Congregation for the Clergy, *Letter on Confession and First Communion*, March 21, 1977.

[28] Paul VI, address to the bishops of New York State during their *ad limina* visit, April 20, 1978.

[29] John Paul II, address to a group of Canadian bishops during their *ad limina* visit, November 17, 1978.

[30] *Redemptor hominis*, no. 20.

[31] *Code of Canon Law* (1983), canon 914.

[32] John Paul II, address to a group of American bishops during their *ad limina* visit, April 15, 1983, no. 5.

[33] Sacred Congregation for the Doctrine of the Faith *Pastoral Norms Concerning the Administration of General Sacramental Absolution*, June 16, 1972, no. XII; these norms are essentially incorporated in the 1983 *Code of Canon Law*, canons 960–963.

[34] Rite of Penance, December 2, 1973, Intro., n. 7.

[35] Paul VI, apostolic exhortation *Gaudete in Domino*, May 9, 1975, part V.

[36] John Paul II, encyclical *Dives in misericordia*, November 30, 1980, nos. 5–6.

[37] J. Escrivá, *Christ Is Passing By* (Chicago and Dublin, 1974), no. 64.

[38] J. Escrivá, *Friends of God*, no. 216.

[39] Council of Trent, session 14, chapter 1: DS 1670; cf. canon 3: DS 1703.

[40] John Paul II, *Letter to Priests* (1983), no. 2.

[41] Cf. John Paul II, address of December 23, 1982, no. 5.

[42] John Paul II, *Letter to Priests* (1983), no. 3.

[43] *Redemptor hominis*, no. 22.

[44] *Presbyterorum ordinis*, no. 13.

[45] *Christus Dominus*, no. 30.

[46] Letter of Cardinal Villot quoted in note 26.

[47] Paul VI, address of April 20, 1978, quoted in note 28.

[48] John Paul II, address of November 17, 1978, quoted in note 29.

[49] *Letter to Priests* (1983), no. 3.

[50] John Paul II, address of April 15, 1983, quoted in note 32, nos. 3-4.

[51] Ibid., no. 6.

[52] Cardinal Humberto Medeiros, pastoral letter for Lent 1981, in *Whatever God Wants: Pastorals and Addresses by His Eminence Humberto Cardinal Medeiros* (Boston, 1984), pp. 317-330.

[53] *Code of Canon Law* (1983), canon 916: "Anyone who is conscious of grave sin may not celebrate Mass or receive the Body of our Lord without previously having been to sacramental confession, unless there is a grave reason and there is no opportunity to confess; in this case the person is to remember the obligation to make an act of perfect contrition, which includes the resolve to go to Confession as soon as possible."

[54] J. Escrivá, February 14, 1975, in S. Bernal, *Msgr. Escrivá de Balaguer: A Profile of the Founder of Opus Dei* (London, 1977), p. 116.

[55] Cf. note 35.

[56] John Paul II, address of December 23, 1982, no. 4.

[57] Ibid., no. 5.

[58] Bull *Aperite portas*, January 6, 1983, no. 5.

[59] Ibid., no. 6.

[60] Ibid., no. 7.

[61] Ibid., no. 8.

[62] Ibid., no. 11.

[63] John Paul II, *Letter to Bishops*, January 25, 1983, no. 5.

[64] *L'Osservatore Romano*, English ed., February 27 to April 24, 1984.

[65] *Aperite portas*, no. 3; cf. *Letter to Priests* (1983), no. 4.

[66] John Paul II, address to priests of the Diocese of Rome, February 17, 1983, no. 3; cf. *Letter to Priests* (1983), no. 4.

[67] *Redemptor hominis*, no. 22.

[68] John Paul II, homily during Mass celebrated in the Basilica of Our Lady of Zapotan, January 30, 1979.

Author's Foreword

In recent years, in connection with the liturgical movement and other new developments pertaining to Catholic piety, there has been much written and also much
discussion about the frequent Confession of venial sins
or, as we commonly say, Confession of devotion. In his
encyclical on the Mystical Body of Christ (*Mystici Corporis*, June 29, 1943), Pope Pius XII turned his attention
to frequent Confession, defended it against those who
were belittling it, and recommended most earnestly that
"pious practice, introduced by the Church under the
guidance of the Holy Spirit." The Pope sets out clearly
the Church's attitude to frequent Confession: "Therefore those among the young clergy who are diminishing
esteem for frequent Confession are to know that the enterprise upon which they have embarked is alien to the
Spirit of Christ and most detrimental to the Mystical
Body of our Savior" (CTS translation, London 1952,
par. 87).

There are, unfortunately, not a few, including even
some Catholics, who have expressed opinions against
frequent Confession and who seem to believe that it
should not be recommended—indeed, that people
should hold back from it.

How different is the attitude of the Church; for the
Code of Canon Law (1917) makes frequent Confession a
duty for candidates for the priesthood (canon 1367.2),
for all clerics (125.1), and for religious (595.1, 3)!

Since the first edition of this work appeared in 1922,

as a result of the difficulties raised against frequent Confession, many new and important points of view on this matter have emerged. From various sources there have come many good and practical suggestions as to how frequent Confession can be made a more vital element of the spiritual life. Therefore it seemed to me to be necessary to undertake a thorough rewriting of the earlier editions, which would take recent developments into account and incorporate these new ideas.

Frequent Confession has been written especially for the many souls in the priesthood and the religious life who are earnestly striving after sanctity and for the many good people who are sincerely trying to work out their salvation in the world. I am firmly convinced that among all these today there is a real need for frequent Confession—and so made as to be fruitful and life-giving, not merely a "practice," not mechanically done, nor done only because it is prescribed by Canon Law or one's religious rule. Hence this book has as its aim to set the practice of frequent Confession on solid foundations, to give it new vigor, to lead to better understanding of it, and to show its high value in the spiritual life.

Abbot Butler of Downside wrote: "The more that educated and intellectual Catholics in their practical religious life throw themselves into the great stream of living Catholicism and partake with simplicity of heart, each one according to his individual spirit, bent, attraction, in the ordinary devotions and pious practices of the poor, the higher will they rise in the religion of the spirit" (*Benedictine Monasticism*, London 1919, p. 306). It seems to me that these words can be applied also to frequent Confession, seeing that it is practiced so much in the Church and that it is so strongly recommended by the Church's highest authority.

—PENTECOST, 1945

PART ONE

FREQUENT CONFESSION

CHAPTER ONE

The Meaning and Purpose
of Frequent Confession

A person may receive the sacrament of Penance frequently for the reason that over and over again he falls into mortal sins and wants to obtain forgiveness for them from God. We are not speaking here of frequent Confession in this sense. What we have in mind is the frequent and regular Confession of a person who in general does not commit mortal sin but rather lives a life of union with God and is bound to him by love. Such a person may, nevertheless, be guilty of many disloyalties and failings. He may have various weaknesses and bad habits and perverse inclinations, and he may have to struggle hard with his inordinate desires and his self-love. It is not a matter of indifference to him that here and there he has acted against his conscience, even though it be in nonessential matters. He is anxious to purify his soul from every stain of sin and from every fault and to keep it pure and to keep his will steadfastly directed toward God. For this reason he goes frequently to Confession, possibly every week. He seeks inner purification and strength of will, new strength to strive after perfect union with God and with Christ.

He knows well that he is in no way bound in conscience to confess the venial sins that he has committed. He knows—for it is the explicit teaching of the Church—that venial sins need not be told in Confession: and this because there are many other means by which they can be forgiven. Such means are all acts of true supernatural contrition, all petitions for the forgiveness of sin, all works undertaken and sufferings borne in a spirit of penance and atonement, all acts of perfect love of God, all works of Christian charity toward neighbor that spring from a supernatural motive—in a word, every work that is done and every sacrifice that is made out of supernatural love. Other means still are the right use of what we call sacramentals, for example, holy water and various liturgical prayers, such as the *Confiteor*. There is, especially, assistance at Holy Mass and the reception of Holy Communion: for, as the Council of Trent says, through Holy Communion we are "purified from our daily faults" (Session XIII, ch. 2). For the soul that is honestly striving, God's mercy has indeed made it very easy to atone for past faults and failings.

If there are so many ways in which the soul can be cleansed from venial sin without recourse to the sacrament of Penance, what meaning or what value has the confession of venial sins? Wherein exactly lies the "profit" of such confession, of which the Council of Trent speaks? For the Council says: "Venial sins, which do not separate man from God and into which we frequently fall, are rightly and with profit accused in Confession, as is the practice of pious Christians" (Session XVII, ch. 5).

(a) *The Advantages of Frequent Confession*

The "profit" of the confession of venial sins comes above all else from the fact that when we go to Confession we receive a sacrament. The forgiveness of sin takes place by the power of the sacrament, that is, by the power of Christ himself. In the sacrament of Penance, says the Council of Trent, "the merits of the death of Christ are applied to those who have sinned after

Baptism" (Session XIV, ch. 1). It should be noted too that it is not upon the sins committed themselves that the action of the sacrament falls but rather upon our interior aversion of heart from sin; it is this that the power of the sacrament takes hold of, as it were, and elevates in order to unite us to God through grace.

Since it is exclusively venial sin that is in question here, the grace bestowed by Confession is not, as in the case where mortal sin is confessed, a new life of grace, the "state of grace"; rather, it is the strengthening and deepening of the supernatural life already existing in the soul and an increase of the love of God. In these circumstances the sacrament is primarily positive in its effects: it strengthens the supernatural life of the soul, increases sanctifying grace, and, along with this, gives actual grace, which stimulates our will to acts of love of God and of contrition for our sins. Such sentiments of love tend to uproot venial sins and cast them out of the soul, just as light dispels and does away with darkness.

The value of the confession of venial sins lies furthermore in this: that the power of the sacrament not merely blots out these sins but also undoes their evil consequences in the soul more fully than is the case when venial sins are forgiven outside Confession. Thus, for instance, when venial sins are forgiven in Confession a greater part of the temporal punishment due to them is forgiven than would be outside the sacrament with the same sentiments of contrition. But especially the sacrament of Penance cures the soul from the weakness that follows venial sin and from the weariness and coldness toward the things of God and the inclination toward worldliness that venial sin brings; it delivers the soul from its reawakened inordinate inclinations and instincts and from the domination of concupiscence: and all this by its sacramental power, in other words, by the power of Christ himself. Moreover, the confession of venial sins gives the soul an interior freshness, a new aspiration and impetus toward self-surrender to God and toward the cultivation of the supernatural life: results that are not usually produced at all when venial sin is forgiven outside Confession.

A very important advantage of the confession of venial sins is that as a rule our examination of conscience and especially our acts of contrition, of purpose, of amendment, and of resolution to atone and do penance are much more carefully made when we go to Confession than is the case of the extra-sacramental forgiveness of venial sin, for example, by means of an ejaculation or by the pious use of holy water. We know quite well what an effort it takes to formulate properly the accusation of our sins for the priest and how intent we must be to elicit a good act of contrition and purpose of amendment and to form the intention to do our penance and atone for our sins. We must consciously and of set purpose apply ourselves to making these acts well.

Indeed, it is only right that we should take this trouble. For these acts of interior aversion from our faults are required not merely as a psychological predisposition for the reception of the sacrament of Penance; they are essential constituent parts of the sacrament. They are necessary for the very existence of the sacrament, and the measure of the effects of the sacrament—of the increase of divine life and of the remission of sin—is determined by them.

Apart from the sacrament of Matrimony, Penance is the most personal of the sacraments. The personal dispositions of the penitent—his personal expression of sorrow, of accusation of sin, and of the desire to atone for it—are absolutely necessary for this sacrament. Its efficacy depends essentially on our personal attitude to the sins we have committed and on our personal turning back to Christ and to God. In the sacrament of Penance these personal acts of penance of ours are elevated; they no longer remain purely personal but are linked with the sufferings and death of Christ, from which the power of the sacrament comes. Here, indeed, we see clearly the great value and advantage of the sacrament of Penance.

What we call the sacramental grace of the sacrament of Penance—the grace that belongs to this sacrament and that is not given and cannot be given by any other sacrament—is sanctifying grace with the special power and function of remedying the debility of soul and the lack of vigor and courage and energy, caused by venial sin, and of strengthening the soul and removing the obstacles that the working of grace encounters in it.

Another important value and advantage of frequent Confession is that in it our venial sins are confessed to the priest as the representative of the Church and thus, in a sense, to the Church itself, to the Christian community. It is true that the person who has committed venial sin remains a living member of the Church. But by his venial sin he has offended not only against God and Christ and against the good of his own soul; he has also acted against the interests of the Christian community, the Church. His sin is a spot and wrinkle (Eph 5: 27) on the garment of the Bride of Christ, an obstacle preventing the charity poured forth in the Church by the Holy Spirit (Rom 5: 5) from flowing freely in all the members. Venial sin does a wrong to the community of Christians and is a failure in charity toward the Church, in which alone are the sources of life and salvation for the Christian. Therefore it can be atoned for in no better way than by being confessed to the representative of the Church, absolved by him, and expiated by the penance he imposes.

(b) *Positive Aim of Frequent Confession*

The usefulness of frequent Confession is not confined to the fact that in this sacrament the faults of which we have been guilty are forgiven and the interior weakness of our soul is cured. Frequent Confession looks not only backward to what was, to our past failings; it looks forward also to the future. Precisely by its frequency it aims at an eminently positive goal: at strengthening and invigorating our will in the struggle to acquire true Christian virtue, to become perfectly pure and pleasing in God's sight, to put the supernatural man in full control, to make the spirit reign over the impulses and passions and weaknesses of the old man.

Frequent Confession helps us to foster ever more within ourselves a Christlike disposition and especially a Christian hatred of everything in us that displeases God. It helps us to develop a spirit of Christian penance and atonement and the desire to make satisfaction for our own sins and for those of others. And from a genuine disposition to do penance there grows a readiness for all the sacrifices and sufferings and difficulties and trials that the Lord may allow to come upon us. These are some of the precious things that the devout and frequent reception of the holy sacrament of Penance will bring us.

(c) *Frequent Confession and Spiritual Direction*

1. As a further advantage of frequent Confession many lay stress on the spiritual direction given by one's confessor. It is a fact that for those who are striving to attain

a high standard in the Christian or religious life spiritual direction is highly desirable and useful, if not, indeed, often morally necessary. Today most people look to their confessor for their spiritual direction. And rightly so. One big reason why the Church prescribes frequent and even weekly confession for priests and seminarians and religious must surely be because by this means the spiritual direction of those who are bound in a special way to seek after Christian perfection is most easily and securely provided for.

According to St. Alphonsus Liguori, one of the principal duties of a confessor is to give spiritual direction to his penitents. However, it would be a mistake to think that spiritual direction is essentially something connected with Confession or with frequent Confession. Nor is it correct to associate Confession with spiritual direction to the extent of almost overlooking the sacramental nature of Confession and putting its usefulness as a means of directing souls in the first place, as indeed sometimes happens. It may be noted too that for religious, both men and women, a good deal of spiritual direction is normally provided by their common religious life, regulated as it is by their rule and by the prescriptions of superiors. The way of life laid down by his rule for the religious is the way he must travel in order to come to God; normally it is along that way that he will find all the means that are necessary to reach the goal of religious life and attain sanctity.

2. Can a person confess again sins—mortal sins or venial sins—that he has already duly confessed? We have already remarked that what is taken hold of by the sacramental power of Confession and elevated is not the sins that we confess but the interior acts of the will by which we turn away from these sins: our sentiments of contrition, of desire to make atonement, and so on.

Now, once a sin has been committed it remains a fact always that sin has been committed, even after it has been fully pardoned. And it is possible for a person again and again to turn away interiorly from such a sin, to condemn it, to be sorry for it, to resolve to avoid it for the future and to amend his life, to do acts of penance for it.

There is no reason why such interior dispositions, as often as they are present, should not be elevated by the power of Christ in the sacrament of Penance and made fruitful of grace. For also in this case, where sins that have already been confessed and forgiven are confessed again, the sacrament produces its essential effects: it increases sanctifying grace, which, from its very nature as the fruit of the sacrament of Penance, blots out sin if such happens to be on the soul. The grace produced by the sacrament of Penance cannot be conceived without reference to sin: to the sin it would take away were the soul in a state of sin. Therefore the words of the priest, "I absolve thee," have their full meaning even when they do nothing but increase grace and do not actually take away sin for the simple reason that there is no sin there to take away. Hence the Church teaches that sins that have already been confessed are "sufficient matter" for Confession (*Code of Canon Law,* 1917, canon 902). And Pope Benedict XI in 1304 declared that it is "salutary" to confess again sins that have been confessed previously (Denzinger, *Enchirid. Symb.*, no. 470).

3. What we mean by frequent Confession should be clear from what has been said so far. Frequent Confession is Confession that is adapted to the effective realization of a twofold aim: the purification of the soul from venial sin and, at the same time, the confirmation of the will in its struggle to attain perfection and closer

union with God. This aim is ordinarily pursued by weekly or fortnightly Confession or by Confession every three or four weeks. The Church also reckons with the fact that people may go to Confession even oftener than once a week (*Code of Canon Law*, 1917, canon 595); while, on the other hand, she permits us to gain all indulgences, even those for which Confession is prescribed as a condition, without going specially to Confession each time, provided we either confess at least twice in the month or receive Holy Communion daily or almost daily (ibid., canon 931).

It follows from all the above that frequent Confession presupposes and demands an earnest striving after purity of soul and virtue and after union with God and with Christ, in other words, a real interior life. The person who is satisfied with merely avoiding mortal sin, who cares nothing about and pays no attention to venial sin and definite unfaithfulness and failings, who has not made up his mind to struggle earnestly against these: such a person is not likely to profit by frequent Confession. In other words, frequent Confession is incompatible with a life of tepidity; indeed, from its very nature it is one of the most powerful means of overcoming tepidity and of keeping it far away. If it is properly practiced, it necessarily forces one to strive after virtue and perfection and to fight against even the smallest deliberate sin or unfaithfulness or negligence.

Perfect souls seek and find in frequent Confession the strength and the courage needed for the pursuit of virtue and for a life lived for God and in union with him. Such people seek before all else perfect purity of soul. They feel deeply sorry if they offend their loving Father by unfaithfulness of any kind. They have always before their eyes Christ, the Bridegroom of their souls, full of beauty and unspotted purity and holiness. They want to share his life, to live it with him, to continue it, to be other Christs. Urged on by their love of the Father and by their love for Jesus, in whose likeness they wish to grow daily, they go frequently to Confession. It is the holy love of Christ and of God that impels such souls to receive the sacrament of Penance frequently. Frequent Confession is, indeed, a necessity for them.

Less perfect souls seek and find in frequent Confession an excellent means to make effective their fight against imperfections, against daily failings, against inordinate inclinations and practices, and especially against spiritual weariness and the danger of discouragement. As a result of their frequent reception of the sacrament of Penance these souls feel that somebody stronger than themselves is fighting and winning in them and with them: Christ our Lord, who has overcome sin and who can and will mightily overcome it in the members of his Mystical Body too.

We can well end this chapter with the words of Pope Pius XII in his encyclical on the Mystical Body of Christ, issued on June 29, 1943: "It is clear that in these deceptive doctrines [of unsound quietism] the mystery of which we are treating becomes directed, not to the spiritual profit of the faithful, but to their unhappy ruin. Equally disastrous in its effects is the false contention that the frequent confession of venial sins is not a practice to be greatly esteemed, and that preference is to be given to that general confession which the Bride of Christ, together with her children united to her in the Lord, makes daily through the priests who are about to go up to the altar of God. That there are many very laudable ways in which these sins can be expiated is perfectly true. But for a constant and speedy advancement in the paths of virtue, we highly recommend the pious practice of frequent Confession, introduced by the Church under the guidance of the Holy Spirit; for by this means we grow in a true knowledge of ourselves and in Christian humility, bad habits are uprooted, spiritual negligence and apathy are prevented, the conscience is purified and the will strengthened, salutary spiritual direction is obtained, and grace is increased by the efficacy of the sacrament itself. Therefore those among the young clergy who are diminishing esteem for frequent Confession are to know that the enterprise upon which they have embarked is alien to the Spirit of Christ and most detrimental to the Mystical Body of our Savior."

CHAPTER TWO

The Practice of Frequent Confession

The question as to what precise method we should follow in the actual making of our frequent Confessions is not an easy one to answer. Here, as in so many other matters, what is good for one is not necessarily good for everybody. We must first of all distinguish two different classes among those who practice frequent Confession.

Many of those who confess frequently live in the midst of the turmoil of life: in the family, the office, the factory, teaching or exercising some other profession, carrying on their work amidst hurry and bustle and fuss. They do, indeed, make an honest attempt to lead a good life and please God. They keep themselves all the time in the state of grace and remain friends of God. But they continually fall into faults of every kind. They go every week or at least every month to Confession. They are truly sorry for their faults and, with the very best dispositions, contritely accuse themselves of them, as well as they can, though perhaps not in an entirely perfect way.

Are we going to say that such confession has no advantages for these souls? Are we going to disturb them on account of the clumsy and awkward way in which they make their confession or, without real necessity, force them to make it otherwise? Should we not, rather, try to help them to make earnest and practical resolutions and to keep up their courage and push forward in spite of failure and so advance in the spiritual life?

The same advice should normally hold good in those years of religious life when more serious faults and failings and unfaithfulness, perhaps even fully deliberate venial sins, still occur. During these years it is to be recommended that Confession should be closely linked with the daily meditation and with the examination of conscience, both general and particular.

Normally, however, as we make progress, a simplifying process goes on continually in our whole spiritual lives. This is true with regard to meditation and examination of conscience and with regard to our whole effort to acquire virtue and lead a life of prayer. Our way of approaching the sacrament of Penance is also subject to this process of simplification. As we advance in the spiritual life, fully deliberate venial sins become less and less frequent and, as a rule, we fall into scarcely anything more than what are called sins of frailty. But now practical difficulties with regard to Confession begin to arise and, indeed, the more the soul grows in purity and union with God, the greater they become.

The following details regarding the method of practicing frequent Confession hold good for both these classes of souls of which we have spoken. We shall begin with the purpose of amendment.

(a) *Purpose of Amendment*

If frequent Confession is to be made not only validly and worthily but in such a way as to be of real positive value for the growth and development of the interior life, there is one guiding principle that must be observed. Whatever faults we tell in Confession, these we must have firmly made up our minds to overcome. Consequently our purpose of amendment is a point of central importance in the practice of frequent Confession.

1. A purpose of amendment is inseparable from genuine contrition; it follows it with absolute necessity as its natural fruit. Being really a part of contrition, the purpose of amendment, like contrition itself, is an essential and strictly necessary constituent part of Confession.

It is worthwhile distinguishing between an *explicit* purpose of amendment and a purpose of amendment *implicitly contained in contrition.* This latter is not a new distinct act of the will, separate from the act of contrition. And it is sufficient for the valid reception of the sacrament of Penance. Therefore if a penitent, before confessing his sins, makes merely a sincere act of contrition without thinking about a purpose of amendment and without formulating such a purpose, his Confession is good and valid because the necessary purpose of amendment is contained implicitly in his contrition.

However, if a person wants his Confession to be really fruitful and so become for him a means to interior progress and sanctity, then an explicit purpose of amendment, distinct from the act of contrition, is desirable. Such an explicit purpose of amendment can be either *general* or *particular.* It is general if it extends to all venial sins or, at any rate, to all the venial sins confessed in the present Confession. The particular purpose of amendment, on the other hand, means a resolve to avoid or at least to fight earnestly against this or that particular venial sin.

When only venial sins have to be confessed, as far as the purpose of amendment goes it is sufficient for the *validity* of the confession to be resolved to avoid or to strive against those venial sins that have been accused or even against *one* of these. Also it suffices to resolve to refrain from a particular kind of venial sin or to avoid as much as possible semi-deliberate venial sins (sins of frailty, as we call them) or at least, through greater fervor, to try to lessen their number. Our purpose of amendment need not be to avoid venial sins absolutely, as it has to be with regard to mortal sins; it is enough to have a purpose to fight against them or to take measures at least to diminish their frequency.

2. Many who practice frequent Confession make the great mistake of having no real purpose of amendment regarding many of the sins they confess. St. Francis de Sales says that it is an abuse to confess a sin in Confession unless one's mind is made up to avoid it in the future or at least to strive earnestly against it *(An Introduction to the Devout Life,* part 2, ch. 19). Unfortunately this abuse frequently becomes a habit, especially in that kind of routine thoughtless Confession in which the same things are confessed time after time without any real effort to make progress, to lessen the number and variety of venial sins, to turn away sincerely from sin and increase in fervor and virtue. There must, indeed, be something wanting here. What is wanting is a purpose of amendment. The penitent has got into the habit of confessing this or that venial sin without ever seriously thinking of striving energetically against it. No doubt he always has a general purpose of amendment or, at any rate, a purpose of amendment implicit in his contrition, and consequently his Confession is valid. But such Confession can scarcely be very fruitful or help very much to build up and develop an interior life. Here, indeed, confessors have a responsibility with regard to those who confess frequently, but the responsibility is not theirs alone; first and foremost it rests on the penitents themselves.

In view of all this, holy souls who are advancing in the spiritual life should not confess in their frequent Confessions any failings or unfaithfulness or sins of frailty that they are not fully resolved to avoid or at least to strive against. Now, it is quite impossible for a person to persevere in concentrating his full powers and attention on a big number of failings and weaknesses at the same time. Therefore our guiding principle here should be: a little, but well done; a little done earnestly and with purpose and perseverance. *Divide and conquer!* People such as those of whom we are speaking should limit their purpose of amendment to very few points, often to one single failing against which they are determined to strive; they should confine it to one particular thing to which they are resolved to pay special attention and on which they wish to concentrate all their energy. In the first place, let them choose that which at the moment is most necessary or important, that which in the circumstances matters most for them. A great deal depends on whether this purpose of amendment is well chosen and well formulated.

These advanced souls must be careful too to have a *positive* purpose of amendment, that is, one that is directed to the practice of some particular virtue. We do not overcome small faults and weaknesses by being continually busied about them and fighting against them but rather by keeping our gaze directed on what is positively good and holy and consciously striving after that. Souls that are really trying to advance aim above all else at developing a pure new love for God and for Christ. And love for God implies love for one's neighbor: a tolerant, forgiving love that tries to help and serve others and make life pleasant for them. These souls strive after purity of life and try to have right motives in all their daily actions; they aim at continual prayer, through which they bring to God and to their Savior everything that befalls them. Love of God and of the Savior makes them strong for the daily sacrifices, big and small; it enables them to be patient and truthful, to bear the burdens of community life, to submit humbly to the Cross in the form of difficult circumstances—sickness, their own weakness and insufficiency, their frequent failure, the trials of the interior life, dryness, interior emptiness and coldness, weariness, indisposition of body, disinclination to pray.

Love is what makes all the difference. "Charity is patient, is kind; charity envieth not, dealeth not perversely, is not puffed up; is not ambitious, seeketh not her own, is not provoked to anger, thinketh no evil, beareth all things, believeth all things, hopeth all things, endureth all things. Follow after charity" (1 Cor 13: 4ff.). In other words: seek after a holy love of God and of Christ, for with love goes every virtue.

Our purpose of amendment must always be something *practical*. And here many fall into error. A person makes a resolution like this, for instance: "I will never again be distracted at prayer." Or "I will never again lose my temper"; "I will never again be irritable"; "I will never again entertain proud thoughts"; and so on. These are resolutions it is quite impossible to carry out, and the person who makes them is only increasing his troubles.

It is much too much to expect that men and women here on earth should not be subject to distractions at prayer or should never lose their tempers, that they should never become irritated by unpleasant or unfair treatment, that they should never be troubled by proud thoughts. What can be expected is that they should not deliberately give way to distractions or irritation, for instance; that as soon as they become conscious of such things they should fight against them. With this in mind, a purpose of amendment that is really practical can be formulated; for example, "As soon as I recognize that I am distracted, I will recollect myself"; "As soon as I recognize that I am becoming irritated, I will make an act of patience or of conformity with God's will"; "Whenever I experience something unpleasant, I will go to our Lord and say 'Lord, help me,' or 'For love of thee, Lord, I will bear this.'" If a person attempts more than this, his purpose of amendment is doomed to failure, and only disappointment and discouragement will result.

Our purpose of amendment must be *adapted to actual circumstances and needs*. It ought to concern a fault that causes trouble, the overcoming of which is important. And it should take into consideration too the interior attraction of grace, which very frequently is connected with some special mystery of the life of Christ or of the liturgy or of the liturgical year, or with some special experience one has had, or with meditation, spiritual reading, or interior illumination.

Our purpose of amendment *need not be*, indeed should not be, *changed* in every Confession. But if it is not changed, it should be renewed and made more firm and more solidly established in every Confession. As a rule, the same purpose of amendment should be retained and renewed in each Confession until the fault against which it is directed has been energetically attacked for some time and its dominance notably shaken. Often it may be necessary to keep the same purpose of amendment for a very long time, as long as certain external circumstances remain unchanged. Certain exterior failings, such as curiosity of the eyes or breaches of silence or uncharitable conversation, must be fought by a special purpose of amendment against them until the contrary habit has been developed. And for this the particular examination of conscience and our daily meditation can help a great deal too.

Our purpose of amendment can also be *directed to certain means* that we wish to take against a particular fault.

Thus, in order to overcome distractions in prayer better, one could resolve to be more faithful in making one's meditation; in order to overcome impatience and criticism of others and want of charity, one could resolve to keep more in the presence of God and to control one's senses.

Let it not be forgotten that our purpose of amendment implies that we *have good will and the resolve to amend at the time we make it*: but that this is quite compatible with the fear, even with the knowledge, that we shall probably fall again, at least into indeliberate faults. We must always take into account the important truth of faith that, even when in the state of grace, we cannot "avoid all venial sins during the whole of life, without a special privilege from God, such as the Church holds our Blessed Lady received" (Council of Trent, Session VI, ch. 23).

The important thing for us is not so much that we never again fall into any faults but rather that we never become indifferent and careless about our faults and failings or about their roots and causes, that we sincerely turn away from them and never come to terms with them, that we always keep on climbing upward to the holy heights of God's love.

(b) *Confession: Telling Our Sins*

1. The Council of Trent emphasizes the fact that venial sins need not be confessed. "Venial sins may rightly and with profit be told in Confession; but they can also be withheld without any fault and expiated by various other means" (Session XIV, ch. 5).

Sins alone can be matter for Confession, and only sins that have been committed after Baptism. What is not a sin cannot be matter for Confession. Thus venial sins that have been freely and knowingly committed can be confessed—deliberate venial sins, as we call them. What we call sins of frailty are also matter for Confession: the sins of which we are guilty in rash moments, on account of some passing excitement, from want of reflection, through forgetfulness or thoughtlessness: sins that are committed without full attention or full deliberation. The number and the aggravating circumstances of venial sins need not be confessed; but it is a good thing in the case of our more serious and deeply rooted faults to make such a reckoning about them and to include it in our accusation. An instance of exaggerating circumstances would be, for example, to show oneself uncharitable immediately after Holy Communion or to show oneself uncharitable toward a benefactor.

The question used to be discussed whether one can or should confess "imperfections"—for example, when we defend ourselves in a situation where it would be more perfect (though not of strict obligation) to remain silent; or when we allow ourselves something it would be better to do without. At present it is customary to confess imperfections also, at least for the reason that generally some negligence underlies the imperfect action and that consequently the knowledge of this latter is useful to the confessor for the direction of the penitent. But really indeliberate and involuntary distractions in prayer, manifestations of impatience, uncharitable thoughts and feelings, aversions, rash judgments, and such things, insofar as they are really indeliberate and involuntary, they are not matter for Confession.

2. Souls devoting themselves earnestly to the spiritual life and especially religious—who by their vocation are pledged to a life of Christian perfection—will gen-

erally, once they have left the initial stage of the spiritual life behind them, as a matter of principle confess those sins and faults against which they have made up their minds to strive deliberately. They will of set purpose, therefore, not confess any and every failing and imperfection into which they may have fallen but only those against which their purpose of amendment is directed. Purpose of amendment and confession (accusation) run parallel. And here also the principle holds: not much and of many different kinds but, rather, a little and well done. *Non multa, sed multum.* Out of their various daily faults and unfaithfulnesses and transgressions such persons will choose one or the other: that which tends to hold its ground obstinately, that which is more consciously and deliberately indulged in, that which causes annoyance to those around them, or that which results from some disordered practice or some inordinate inclination or passion.

This limited accusation is to be specially recommended to those who, in spite of all their striving, forget themselves now and then and are guilty of faults committed through force of habit or faults of a more serious kind arising from their individual temperament. It is to be recommended to those who feel sluggish and languid and without the inner strength and the real desire to strive after virtue; to those who are in danger of becoming lukewarm and careless; to those who have great difficulty in ridding themselves of certain faults; and, finally, to those who easily become worried by doubts as to whether they have had sufficient contrition for the sins they have confessed.

"We only substitute our own notions for the law of God insofar as we consider it our duty to recite a whole litany of venial sins with all particulars and details. To go into all these details is quite unnecessary. All that results from it is the anxiety and scruples that come entirely from having omitted, when it was impossible to do otherwise, something that could have been passed over without any fault whatsoever on our part" (Lehen, *Weg zum inneren Frieden*). In the effort to confess all our venial sins, there is, besides much ignorance and lack of understanding, a good deal of self-seeking and pride. The penitent wants to be satisfied with his performance and wants to be able to convince himself that he has told everything that could be told. Thus many souls deceive themselves by thinking that once a thing is confessed, everything is all right. What a pernicious error!

Knowledge of the root causes of venial sins, especially of one's predominant fault, and of the occasions of certain faults can be useful for the confessor. It is a good thing to speak of these matters in Confession from time to time.

3. In practice there are many ways of making our accusation well and fruitfully and of simplifying our practice of frequent Confession and giving it more solid foundations.

A penitent may confess all or at least the more important failings of which he has been guilty since his last Confession. Many do this and indeed rightly and with profit.

For more advanced souls, however, who are earnestly striving after holiness, either in the world or in the priesthood or in the religious life, we believe some of the following methods are advisable.

(i) The Confession can be made to center on one definite fault that has occurred since the previous Confession, taking a form something like this: "I have deliberately judged and spoken uncharitably. During my whole past life I have sinned much against fraternal charity in thought and in word by uncharitable judgments and I now accuse myself of all these sins of my whole life. I accuse myself also of all the other sins and faults of which I have been guilty before God." This is a simple and very fruitful way of confessing, provided the penitent takes the trouble to excite himself to sincere contrition. From such contrition will come the clear and concrete purpose of amendment: "I am going to see to it that I overcome this habit of (deliberately) judging and speaking uncharitably and that I get rid of it altogether."

(ii) A second method of confessing is to make the accusation center on one of the commandments or on some inordinate passion or practice or inclination: on some one particular point that at the moment is important for the interior life. Then we can proceed something like this: "I am easily irritated. I lose my temper quickly with other people over various things. I talk and criticize and allow aversions and bad humor to develop in me. I accuse myself also of having sinned often in this way in my past life. And I accuse myself of all the other sins and failings of which I have been guilty before God." This, likewise, is a simple and fruitful way of practicing frequent Confession. It presupposes and demands that the penitent for a fairly long time devote his attention and efforts to one definite fault or to the root cause of certain faults or at least to some point that is important for his interior life. Here also contrition is of the greatest moment. This second kind of accusation makes it relatively easy for the confessor to give the penitent individual treatment and help him along in his efforts.

(iii) Finally, Confession can take the form of accusing oneself of all the sins of one's life, against such and such a commandment, for instance: "I have sinned frequently through impatience, lack of self-control, sensuality, acting from caprice. I accuse myself also of all the other sins of my whole life, mortal and venial."

From what has been said it follows that the person who wants to practice frequent Confession properly and get the best results from it must keep good order within the household of his soul. He must be clear as to what is important or essential for him. He must know his weak points and purposefully get to work on himself. If then the confessor for his part, with understanding and with a holy zeal for the spiritual development of his penitent, purposefully cooperates and helps him along, frequent Confession will become a most valuable means for advancing in the interior life and growing in the likeness and spirit of Christ.

(c) *Examination of Conscience*

1. Our examination of conscience for the reception of the sacrament stands in the closest relation to the practice of examination of conscience in general.

The masters of the spiritual life, from the time of the ancient monks right up to our own day, have always regarded daily examination of conscience as an essential element in a life of true Christian piety. Nevertheless, in certain Catholic circles today there are those who want to hear nothing about detailed examination of conscience and who have no time at all for the "particular examination of conscience," as it is called. For this latter they would substitute just "a simple glance" at the state of the soul. They overlook the fact that, at least for beginners, it is absolutely necessary to go into details if they want to know their faults and the cause of them, if they want to get to know their various passions and inordinate interior dispositions with a view to correcting them. It is precisely beginners who are liable to the danger of being satisfied with a superficial glance that leaves inordinate passions and practices undisturbed.

As St. Pius X once remarked: "What a pity if in this connection also the words of Christ were to the point: 'The children of this world are wiser in their generation than the children of light!' With what diligence do we see the latter attending to their affairs! How frequently they compare their profits and their losses! How exact and careful is their bookkeeping!"

The Church makes daily examination of conscience obligatory for clerics and religious (*Code of Canon Law*, 1917, canons 125 and 592) and expressly rejects the tenet of Molinos that "not to be able to reflect on one's own defects is a grace from God" (Denzinger, *Enchirid. Symb.*, no. 1230). And it was Madame de Guyon, the Quietist, who believed that it was enough simply to "let God's light shine on oneself." It is significant too that many modern writers strongly urge a kind of natural particular examination of conscience as part of a purely natural and human self-formation.

2. Writers on the spiritual life rightly emphasize that examination of conscience is absolutely necessary for the purification of the soul and for progress in virtue. Without regular examination of conscience we never get to know our faults properly. Rather, they increase; evil inclinations and inordinate passions become stronger and may seriously threaten the life of grace. Especially, it will be impossible for charity to develop fully in us.

There are many different ways of practicing examination of conscience. It can have as its aim the discovery of those venial sins—we prescind here from mortal sin—that are fully deliberate. Or it may aim at the discovery of our less deliberate or barely deliberate sins of frailty. Or, finally, it may try to find out how we could and ought to correspond better with God's graces. It is clear in any case that we can make our examination of conscience well and fruitfully only with the help of divine grace.

The general examination of conscience passes under review all the happenings of the day that has gone by: thought, feelings, words, and deeds. When this examination of conscience is made regularly it is not very difficult; a person usually knows his customary failings, and so he discovers without much trouble whatever faults he may have committed in the course of the day. If any unusual lapse has occurred to one who is earnestly striving after virtue, it will stand out and worry him continually. People who are genuinely trying to lead a holy life need in no way be petty in this self-examination. The act of contrition in our examination of conscience is much more important. It is through it that our examination of conscience can always be improved and invigorated. From true contrition will come a purpose of amendment; and this purpose of amendment will generally go to form part of our purpose of amendment in Confession.

The general examination of conscience is supplemented by the particular examination of conscience. This latter concerns itself over a fairly long period with some particular fault that one wishes to eradicate or with some particular virtue that one wishes to acquire. In selecting faults for attack, we ought to begin with exterior faults by which those around us are annoyed or irritated. Then we can proceed to interior faults: our own faults of character, the weak points in our makeup. When we reach the stage at which the fault occurs only very seldom or only on certain special occasions, we ought to change our examination of conscience to reckoning up positive acts of some virtue.

As we make progress in the spiritual life our particular examination of conscience will tend more and more to take on this positive form; its practice will mean the confirmation of our will in the pursuit of a certain virtue, together with prayer to God for constancy and perfection in this virtue, for example, love of God, fraternal charity, the spirit of faith, humility, prayerfulness. Usually too our purpose of amendment in Confession should have some relation to the subject of our particular examination of conscience. Consequently, we can see that the particular examination of conscience is most important for all pious and zealous souls, especially in the positive form just mentioned, which continually keeps the will active in the practice of virtue.

3. It is not enough only to get to know the acts in which we fail. It is equally important, even more important, to explore our interior attitudes and dispositions. For this purpose the so-called "habitual" examination of conscience is to be recommended: a quick look at our interior state, often repeated; a glance to see what feeling or inclination of heart is predominant at the moment.

Among the many feelings that crowd the human heart and assail it, there is always *one* feeling that dominates, that gives the heart its direction, so to speak, and determines its mood. At one time it is the need for recognition by others, at another time fear of blame or of humiliation or suffering, at another time jealousy or embitterment on account of some injustice suffered, at still another time some suspicion or some disordered desire regarding our work or our health. Or again it may be a certain state of spiritual inertia and discouragement on account of certain difficulties or some failure or some other experience.

This predominant feeling can, however, also be a movement of love for God, a compelling desire to make sacrifices, a glowing zeal for God's interests. It can be joy in the service of God, in submission to God, in humiliation, in the desire for mortification and self-surrender to God. "Where is my heart?" What is the prevailing disposition that determines its attitude, the real mainspring that keeps all the rest of its movement going? It may, perhaps, be some long-existent tendency: some attachment or bitterness or aversion. It may be just a momentary impression, but one so deep and strong that it has affected the heart for long afterward. In the "habitual" examination of conscience we ask ourselves: "Where is my heart?" And thus, often during the day, we uncover the disposition and inclination of our heart at the moment and so penetrate to its central core, from which our various words and deeds and activities issue. We discover the chief wellsprings of good and evil within ourselves.

This discovery is very useful for our general and particular examination of conscience and for our examination of conscience in preparation for Confession. It shows us what is important or essential in our pursuit of perfection; it keeps us continually contrite; it fills us with thankfulness if we find that our interior dispositions are rightly ordered; it makes us pray for grace and strength. We discover what we ought to accuse ourselves of in Confession and what our purpose of amendment ought to be. In general, we come to understand how, by means of this habitual, oft-repeated interior examination, we can set on solid foundations our general examination and our particular examination.

4. Our examination of conscience for frequent Confession need not extend to all our faults since our last Confession. First and foremost we should consider

the purpose of amendment made in our last Confession and the subject of our particular examination and see whether and how well we have tried to carry out our resolves. Should it be that in the course of the week (or whatever time has elapsed since our last Confession) something very unusual has happened, some rather serious fault has been committed, this will stand out in our conscience. And our daily general examination of conscience will ensure always that we do not overlook our ordinary daily faults. Consequently, it is not necessary in our examination of conscience for Confession to search out in detail each and every venial sin since our last Confession. In saying this, of course, we are taking it for granted that our examination of conscience for frequent Confession presupposes and indeed requires the practice of the general and particular examinations and the above-mentioned "habitual" examination, as well.

"Venial sins can be withheld in Confession without any fault and expiated by various other means" (Council of Trent, Session XIV, ch. 5). If, then, venial sins need not be confessed, it follows that we are perfectly free not to confess them at all or to confess only those we wish. And so, if I have only venial sins on my soul, strictly speaking I have examined my conscience sufficiently as soon as I discover any venial sin at all committed at any time in my life. I have no obligation to examine my conscience with regard to all the venial sins committed since my last Confession. Catholic moral theology teaches that in the examination of conscience before Confession an extraordinary diligence is not necessary "even if such diligence would discover more sins." Moreover, "if a person knows that he has not committed any mortal sin since his last Confession, he is not strictly obliged to examine his conscience at

all; it suffices that he finds sufficient matter for absolution" (Gopfert, III, no. 119).

In examining our conscience it is important that we
distinguish between what is more necessary and what is
less necessary, between what is essential and what is not
essential, between what is important and what is unimportant. In the course of a particular week some one
matter may happen to become of great importance. It
may be something that is the occasion of a fault for us,
or it may be an especially strong inordinate impulse or
some situation that demands special watchfulness or
that is the cause of bitterness, aversion, and so on.

The more our examination of conscience is confined
to important points and brought into realization with
our purpose of amendment and our accusation, the
more fruitful it will be. Therefore those who confess
frequently have no need to examine their conscience
every time on each and all of the Ten Commandments
of God or on all the items in the "Examination of Conscience" usually found in prayer books.

(d) *Contrition*

1. As regards the question of contrition when we confess only venial sins (together with, perhaps, other venial or even mortal sins that have been confessed
previously), the same principles hold as for contrition
for venial sins in general. Without contrition there can
be no forgiveness.

The matter to which the contrition required in frequent Confession extends can only be that which is matter for accusation and for absolution, namely, sin, the
known and deliberate transgression of the law of God.
What is not a sin cannot be matter for contrition—even
though, perhaps, it can and should be regretted.

For the valid and licit reception of the sacrament of Penance, what we call attrition, or imperfect contrition, is the least that is required, and it suffices. This contrition springs from supernatural motives: the motive of the fear of punishment in this life (for example, withdrawal of graces, failure to reach the stage in the spiritual life we could and should reach) and hereafter (postponement of our admission to Heaven and a lesser degree of eternal happiness than we could otherwise have had).

It would be an exaggeration to say that in general we can neglect these imperfect and rather selfish motives of contrition. But we should not remain content with them; we should rather try deliberately to have perfect contrition. This latter rises above considerations of self and of one's own gain and loss and advantage and disadvantage and thinks only of God: God, whom we wrong by sinning and whose commandments, honor, interests, and desires we put in the second place, second to our own inclinations and whims, when we commit even venial sins. We should remember always, of course, that the important thing in contrition, perfect or imperfect, is not our feelings but our will—so that our attitude is: "Would that I had never sinned. Would that I had never thought or said or done or omitted such and such a thing."

2. When a person has only venial sins to tell in Confession, the Confession is valid if he has contrition for one single venial sin that he confesses or for one particular kind of venial sin, even though he mentions other venial sins for which he has no contrition. Furthermore, it suffices to have contrition in a general way for the negligence and carelessness with which one has given way to venial sins or for taking no notice of semi-deliberate faults and not trying to prevent them.

However, the penitent who confesses frequently is not concerned merely with making a *valid* Confession; he wants especially to make a good and fruitful Confession that will help him effectively in his pursuit of holiness. If frequent Confession is to fulfill this purpose for him, he must take very seriously the axiom that without contrition there is no forgiveness of sin. And from this there follows another axiom that is of fundamental importance for him: only those venial sins should be confessed for which one has real and sincere contrition.

There is what we call "universal contrition." By this we mean sorrow for and loathing of the sins of our whole past life. This universal contrition is of the very greatest importance in the practice of frequent Confession. In every Confession we must deliberately try to extend our contrition to each and every sin, mortal and venial, of our whole past life, and make every effort to excite ourselves to a really good act of contrition for them all. This contrition should be sovereign, even with regard to the smallest sins and unfaithfulness, in the sense that we look on sin of any kind as the greatest of all evils and that we detest it, more than anything else, with the whole force of our will.

It is obvious, of course, that we can excite ourselves to contrition again and again for sins of which we have already repented and for which we have been forgiven. Indeed, in a certain sense, it is our duty to be continually sorry for our past sins; for, as St. Thomas Aquinas says, "it must always remain a source of regret to us that we have sinned" (*Summa theologica*, III, q. 84, art. 8). If we were ever to sanction our past sins or approve of them, we should thereby, as he further remarks, sin again. Therefore, whenever we go to Confession we ought to consider it most important to excite ourselves to a deep and sincere contrition extending to the sins of our whole past life. The more seriously we try to have this contrition, the more surely shall we arrive at that state of compunction of heart which is so important for the interior life and which precisely should be the fruit of frequent Confession. Such universal contrition is to be recommended most strongly to those who confess frequently and this for a twofold reason.

First of all, it will ensure that we make a real act of contrition. Some little failing since our last Confession or some single venial sin of our past life that we tell over and over again is, very often, scarcely enough to make us recognize the full meaning of sin and awaken in us intense and perfect sentiments of sorrow for having offended God. But it will be quite otherwise if in one glance we see all the sins and failings of our whole past life together. We can then easily excite in ourselves sentiments of loathing and hatred for what we have done, sentiments of sorrow for having treated God so badly and for having been so ungrateful to him, and sentiments of aversion from sin with the firm resolution to avoid it in future and to make atonement for it.

A second reason for recommending this universal contrition so strongly is that it is not in keeping with the reverence due this holy sacrament to confess, along with venial sins for which one is really sorry, others for which there is no real contrition.

It is clear, of course, that with this universal contrition for all the sins of our life we must combine contrition for the single sins and failings to which we are particularly prone at the moment and about which we are most concerned: contrition for faults against charity, for other more serious failings, for deeply rooted obstinate faults that stem from our predominant passion or from some very strong disordered inclination or habit.

Contrition such as has been described will help greatly to give life and depth to our practice of frequent Confession and will be a safeguard against routine.

3. The sacrament of Penance is a most personal sacrament. And this is true too in the sense that in Confession our personal realization of our sins and faults plays a decisive role. The more we raise ourselves up to God, the more we shall acquire a knowledge of our secret faults and of the latent impulses of our corrupt hearts. As the soul becomes more closely united with God it begins to understand better the saying of St. John: "If we say that we have no sin, we deceive ourselves" (1 Jn 1: 8). It acquires a deeper understanding of God's holiness and purity and develops a most delicate sensitivity regarding the slightest departure from God's will or from what God desires or claims. It becomes very conscious of the way it has injured others spiritually by word, deed, or omission. It recognizes what sins of omission are and in what innumerable ways we can sin by omission. It comes to understand what it means to misuse a grace and recognizes that if those misused graces had been properly used the whole Church and many souls would have benefited.

The tender conscience of a holy soul is something great and noble. On such a soil contrition will thrive— sentiments of compunction that will make the frequent reception of the sacrament of Penance a necessity and a blessing.

(e) *Satisfaction: Sacramental Penance*

1. Satisfaction is the undertaking of penitential works (prayer, fasting, almsgiving) with the purpose of obtaining remission of the temporal punishment due to sin. When works of penance are imposed by the priest in

the sacrament of Penance they become a sacramental satisfaction that remits the temporal punishment by the power of the sacrament. Such sacramental satisfaction is better and more effective than non-sacramental penance, that is, penance imposed or freely undertaken apart from the sacrament of Penance. The greater penances we have imposed on us in the sacrament of Penance and are ready to undertake, the more securely and fully we shall cancel the debt of temporal punishment that generally remains after the guilt of sin has been forgiven and the more we shall shorten Purgatory for ourselves.

2. As regards the acceptance and performance of our penance, the same principles hold for frequent Confession as for any other Confession. They are as follows:

(i) The penitent is bound in conscience to accept the penance imposed by the confessor and to perform it.

(ii) It is not necessary that the penance be performed before absolution is given, nor even that it should be performed before receiving Holy Communion after Confession.

(iii) Even if a person yields to deliberate distractions while reciting a prayer given as a penance, he nevertheless fulfills the penance imposed and performs the sacramental satisfaction. *deserving of blame*

(iv) If one, either culpably or inculpably, forgets what penance was given him, he is not obliged to repeat the Confession. If he thinks that the confessor still remembers the penance, he may go back to him and ask him what it was, though he is not obliged to do this. However, the holy zeal that impels us to practice frequent Confession will impel us also, in a case where we cannot return and ask the confessor, to impose a suitable penance on ourselves.

(v) If the confessor forgets to give us a penance—and this can happen—we should remind him. Otherwise, we should impose a penance on ourselves.

3. It is in keeping with the spirit of frequent Confession that we should accept and put up with the suffering and sacrifices of daily life and the burdens that our work and the fulfillment of our duty entail, with the express purpose of making satisfaction for our sins. In the sacrament of Penance we become, according to the words of St. Thomas Aquinas, "united with our Lord suffering for our sins." When we go to Confession we want to share in the death sentence that our Lord underwent on account of sin; we want to carry out this death sentence on ourselves and have it carried out on us by actual death with Christ. This death with Christ is accomplished by means of a constant spirit of penance with regard to our past sins, for which we wish to make satisfaction.

But this spirit of penance is at the same time directed toward the future insofar as it makes us strong and ready to bear bravely the privations and sufferings and difficulties and troubles of life and to accept the crosses that come to us in a spirit of atonement and in union with the expiatory suffering and death of Christ our Lord. Such a spirit of penance means that we have a continual sorrow of soul for the sins we have committed, together with the desire to make atonement for them and to rise in spite of them to the heights of virtue and of the love of God. This disposition to do penance and to feel intensely displeased at our past sins and to take pains to overcome sin is of fundamental importance for a truly Christian life.

"Do penance!" (Mt 3: 2; Mk 1: 15). Penance is the road to the Kingdom of Heaven and the entrance door thereto, and without it we can neither get to Heaven nor enter therein. Penance makes us humble and reverent toward God. If the spirit of penance is strong in us, our prayer and our reception of the sacraments will be more zealous and more reverential and more effective. We shall grow ever more grateful to him who forgives us and lifts us up out of sin. We shall understand the truth of Christ's words: the creditor will be loved most by that debtor "to whom he forgave most" (Lk 7: 43). The spirit of penance makes us humble toward others also and gentle and kind and ready to forgive. It creates in us a delicacy of conscience and a steadfastness against every kind of sin and disorder. If the spirit of penance is alive in us, it will open up the sources of joy and interior freedom for us.

"By their fruits you shall know them" (Mt 7: 16, 20). "Every good tree bringeth forth good fruit" (Mt 7: 17). The good tree is frequent Confession. Its fruit is the spirit of penance, the disposition to do penance. From this the confessor, as well as the penitent himself, can tell in any particular case how the practice of frequent Confession is succeeding: whether the Confessions are being made well and fruitfully or whether they are not being made well. Whenever frequent Confession is properly understood and practiced with full earnestness, it always produces the spirit of penance and impels us to works of atonement and satisfaction in union with our Lord, who made atonement for our guilt.

CHAPTER THREE

Spiritual Director, Confessor, and Penitent

1. As a rule, all those who practice frequent Confession are seeking, as well as the essential fruits of the sacrament, direction in the spiritual life. And rightly so. We all feel, indeed, that some spiritual direction is necessary for us. "Beginners who are just coming out of Egypt and trying to free themselves from their inordinate passions need a Moses to lead them. The more advanced, who are following Christ closely and wish to taste the freedom of the children of God, need somebody representing Christ whom they can obey in simplicity of heart" (St. John Climacus).

Who would wish to be his own guide along the paths of the interior life, paths that are full of difficulty and responsibility and at the same time so mysterious and dark? "The man who is his own teacher is the pupil of a fool" (St. Bernard). Indeed, many zealous souls have fallen into error owing to lack of guidance: for the ways of the interior life not clear and obvious to everybody. Besides, the more perfectly the Christian life is lived, the more sacrifice and renunciation and effort are called for, and, consequently, the greater is the danger of deception that it brings. The soul needs a trusty guide who will keep its courage up, urge it on anew, solve its doubts, and help it along in time of discouragement and difficulty.

The interior life consists especially in having the right spirit in all our actions and thoughts and in our whole attitude to life. It consists in the readiness to see everything with the eyes of faith and to act always from supernatural motives. But the great weakness even of pious and zealous souls is that they easily allow themselves to be guided by purely natural reasons and judgments and by merely human motives. Therefore, they generally need guidance to keep their minds directed all the time toward the heights known to us only by faith and to ensure that they act from truly supernatural motives. Nowadays, this guidance is obtained normally from the confessor in the sacrament of Penance. We know, however, that ultimately it is the Holy Spirit who guides the soul. The spiritual director plays the same role with regard to the penitent as the mother who stretches out her hand to the tottering child who cannot yet walk properly, in order to help him to keep his balance. The director urges on the penitent and stimulates him to heed the attraction of grace and to follow it, and he sees to it that his penitent does not turn aside from the way of grace and go on a wrong path.

2. There are different kinds of spiritual direction, suitable for different circumstances. The spiritual direction of beginners is not the same as that of those who are more advanced; and the spiritual direction of the latter will differ again from that of very perfect souls. One kind of spiritual direction is called for in dealing with scruples, another in dealing with interior trials, questions of vocation, and so on. "Hardly anyone is a good director for all, and not often for one person all his life long" (F. W. Faber, *Growth in Holiness*, London, 1936, p. 309). A suitable spiritual director is, indeed, a great blessing for a soul.

In general, changing spiritual directors is a bad thing. But at the same time it is an exaggeration to represent such changing as the greatest evil in the spiritual life and to say that it is tantamount to eternal perdition for the soul! Father Faber is quite right when he expresses the opinion that it is by no means desirable that we should depend too scrupulously on our spiritual director. "When we have lost our liberty and ease with him, he has lost his grace for us; and all this without fault on either side. Spiritual direction must be free as air and fresh as the morning sun. Neither temptation nor scruple, neither mortification nor obedience, must be able to infuse into it one element of bondage. The moment they do, let us break the direction and take the consequences. For the end of spiritual direction in all stages of the interior and mystical life is one and single and invariable, and it is liberty of spirit" (*Growth in Holiness*, p. 311).

3. The penitent owes his director a holy reverence, for the latter is for him the representative of God, clothed with God's authority with regard to the holiest and most intimate interests of his soul. Such a holy and supernatural reverence will be a safeguard too against any interior or exterior disorder that could creep into the relationship between the spiritual director and his penitent.

With this spiritual and childlike reverence there should go a childlike trust and complete candor, which will lay bare to the director all the good and evil of one's interior life. Furthermore, the penitent should be docile and obedient to his director. Nevertheless, the obedience due to a spiritual director is not at all the same as the obedience a religious subject shows to his legitimate superiors. A false conception of the obedience due a spiritual director has often misled souls, causing them to indulge in a false feeling of security, almost as if they had handed over their consciences entirely to the care of the director and had no further need to take any initiative in spiritual things themselves. Such people behave as if they themselves were free from all responsibility, as if they could make their confessor responsible for things that really have to be settled between themselves and God, as if they could and must now give up all independence and merely follow the instructions of their confessor in everything.

That a person should consult his director about important matters of the interior life goes without saying. Our sins and imperfections, the strength of our passions, our disordered inclinations, the temptations and secret whisperings of the evil one, our daily order of time, our interior disturbance, and so forth: we should submit all these to him insofar as is necessary to enable him to judge the state of our soul and advise us and help us. But at the same time each one must face up to the ordinary decisions of everyday life and must be willing to take the responsibility for them on his own shoulders.

Our dealings with our spiritual director should be confined to that which is really necessary. We should not trouble him with things that have nothing to do with his office. Nor should we submit our ideas to him until we have fully discovered whether they are well founded and whether we can justify them before God and in conscience. We should not prolong our consultation or our confession more than is necessary, nor should we try to induce our confessor to talk a great deal. The spiritual life develops slowly, and there is no need for new advice every day—unless we are the kind of people who strike out in a new direction every day and so turn their so-called spiritual life into a constantly changing game in which new experiments are all the time being made.

We should guard against taking up too much of the confessor's or spiritual director's time, especially when there are still others waiting for his help.

Do not talk about your confession or your confessor. The latter is most strictly bound to silence. What he has laid down for his penitent to meet a very special situation is often repeated by the latter out of its context. Talk of this kind degenerates all too easily into unfair treatment of the confessor and causes much harm.

4. "St. Paul was quite willing to solve problems of conscience, but he did not regard it as a Christian ideal that we should be continually putting questions to others and relying on their authority. A constant desire for direction, an irresolute outlook that is always hankering after decisions by ecclesiastical authority, an uneasy clinging to the stole of one's confessor or director: such attitudes would be for him proof that a person had not yet come of age and lacked a sense of responsibility. To be like that may be natural in a child, but it is unworthy of an adult Christian.

"In the Epistle to the Ephesians St. Paul sets out as the aim of all pastoral work 'the perfecting of the saints [that is, of Christians] for the work of the ministry, for the edifying of the body of Christ; until we all meet into the unity of faith and of the knowledge of the Son of God, unto a perfect man, unto the measure of the age of the fullness of Christ; that henceforth we be no more children tossed to and fro, but may in all things grow up in him who is head, even Christ' (Eph 4: 12–15). This maturity of which the Apostle speaks refers of course to the energy and moral steadfastness with which we must face the world around us. But it refers even more to the independence of judgment and sure knowledge of Christian teaching that protects the individual from errors and distorted ideas. The Apostle of the Gentiles is, therefore, no supporter of that short-sighted spirituality which sees in dependence in religious matters a specially clear expression of the spirit of 'thinking with the Church' (*sentire cum Ecclesia*) and which thinks it a good thing that the penitent should turn to his confessor for advice in every little difficulty" (Adam, *Spannungen*).

CHAPTER FOUR

Conscience

We have within us what we call our conscience. We know it as a holy and inviolable power to which we must bow; as a mysterious voice that tells us what we must do and what we must avoid, what is allowed and what is not allowed; a voice that authorizes and approves our decisions and actions, or that, on the other hand, repudiates and condemns them and reproaches us whenever we have acted against its dictates.

1. Conscience lays down a law for us, a definite norm and rule for our moral life. This law is, ultimately, the expression of the law-giving will of God, and it binds therefore under strict obligation. It tells me what is required of me by God's holy will, what is allowed or not allowed by God. It tells me that I must do such a thing or not do it, that I must do it this way or some other way. It sets down an eternal, unchangeable law, ordained by God: a law that orders my every action toward God as toward my final end. This eternal law (*lex eterna*) is the wellspring and source of all other laws: of the natural law; of the positive divine law of the Old Testament and of the New Testament; and of positive human law, ecclesiastical and civil, made by man, in which the natural law and positive divine law find their completion.

Law is an exterior and objective norm of behavior. There is, however, an interior proclamation of the law in every man's heart, telling him each instant what he must do or leave undone; and this proclamation is made by our conscience. It is a judgment pronounced by the practical reason; not a judgment about an event or a fact, but about whether we ought or ought not to do something—about whether we may or may not do it. Because it is a judgment of the practical reason, conscience is an intellectual act. That, however, does not prevent it from being influenced by other factors also: by our various inclinations and passions and instincts and feelings and by the will. Nevertheless, conscience in its essence remains always an act of the practical reason telling us authoritatively what we have to do or avoid here and now.

Conscience is holy and inviolable: like a consecrated altar or a consecrated chalice. It is, therefore, something before which we must stand in awe. Why is it holy? Because it is most intimately connected with God. It is God's voice within us, calling us and admonishing us, warning us or urging us on, commending us or reproving us. Therefore conscience binds us, puts us under a strict obligation, so that it is not lawful for us to disobey its commands or prohibitions. It orders us and binds us with the authority of God, who speaks through it. The man who acts against his conscience or who induces another to do so acts against the majesty and sovereign rights of God. And conscience itself, because it is holy, must condemn such usurpation of the rights of another.

2. Here we must touch on a difficulty that is frequently brought up. Conscience is holy and always binding; yet at the same time it can be erroneous. If conscience were the direct voice of God, certainly it could never be wrong. The basis of conscience, namely, the innate capability of the practical reason to apprehend the first principles of morality, is indeed not subject to error. It is perfectly clear to everybody that "we must avoid evil and do good." From this basic principle, with the help of experience and instruction and study,

we build up gradually a system of morality, and what we call conscience develops; that is, we make individual judgments on the morality of our personal actions here and now and feel ourselves under obligation with regard to them.

Because both the system of morality thus built up and the individual judgments of our conscience depend on human sources of knowledge, which are subject to error, they both are themselves subject to error in many ways. Consequently, a person's conscience can be so badly deceived about something that he has no chance whatever of dispelling his error: what we call "invincible error."

There is also such a thing as "vincible error," error that a person can dispel if he takes reasonable trouble. In this case, as well as in the judgment regarding the licity or illicity of the action, there is at the back of the mind a suspicion that one's conscience is wrong, a feeling that the matter ought to be examined further. Here, consequently, we cannot simply regard the dictate of our practical reason as the voice of God and stop there. What must we do? We must dispel the (vincible) error insofar as this is possible: by reflecting further, by asking somebody, by prayer.

But it is a different matter when the error is invincible. Here too the principle holds: "All that is not faith is sin" (Rom 14: 23), that is, anything one does that is not justified by a sincere personal conviction that it is right and lawful is sinful. One may and, indeed, must follow an invincibly erroneous conscience. For the person in error it can make an objectively good action morally wrong; and it can make what is objectively sinful not only allowable but even obligatory.

To act morally right a person must always be sure that what he has decided to do is lawful; in other words, he may never act when he is in doubt as to the licity of a proposed action. Should it happen that, when one is trying to form a judgment as to whether a certain action is morally lawful or not, serious reasons present themselves both for and against the licity of the action, then he is not permitted to act in this state of doubt. A person doing so would be deliberately putting himself in the danger of sinning. He must first of all "form a certain conscience," that is, he must arrive at a judgment that is certain with regard to the licity or illicity of the action under consideration. A person can generally do this by earnest reflection on the matter, by imploring God's help in prayer, by asking advice from conscientious men, or by seeking enlightenment in books.

3. Conscience is a judgment of the practical reason. This latter includes our natural reason, which draws its knowledge from the world around us and from our own experience, and our reason as enlightened by faith and by the knowledge drawn from supernatural revelation. Insofar as conscience depends on knowledge—both natural knowledge and the knowledge provided by faith—it can develop in breadth and depth and clarity and sureness. Insofar as it is a question of conscience applying universal truths and universal laws to the actual details of daily life, there is also great scope for development. It should be noted that our conscience, in its perceptions and judgments, is always subject to the influence of our feelings and desires, of our moods of joy or of anxiety, of our aspirations and fears. We all know from our own experience and from that of others how easily human feelings and longings can lead us in another direction from that in which conscience tells we should go. It is very important that our conscience, even insofar as it is subject to the influence of our feelings and of the will, should be formed and developed

so as to judge our actions with the greatest possible correctness and objectivity.

The formation of development of our conscience may be said to have two different stages. At first conscience functions in a rather negative way, chiefly in connection with our "examination of conscience." In this stage it is concerned primarily with guilt and sin, though it takes cognizance too of the motives and roots from which our sins spring. But anyone who is really in earnest about the interior life will want to do more than this. He will endeavor to develop his conscience in such a way that it will give him positive guidance in every department of his life. For this purpose he will aim at attaining a high level of Christian wisdom in his moral knowledge and at cultivating his sense of duty to a degree of conscientiousness that will be ready for every sacrifice. Or, approaching the matter in another way, he will make Christ our Lord, the incarnate image of the living God, his model in all things and the all-holy will of God the guiding principle of his life.

This development of conscience is an essential part of the religious and moral formation of a Christian. It goes on almost unnoticed, unsystematically, day by day: in prayer, spiritual reading, study of the Scriptures, and in the reception of the sacraments. Nowadays, however, many religious and moral truths and principles almost necessarily fall into oblivion under the pressure of the worldly, secularized, unchristian way of thinking that prevails around us, and the image of the God-man whom we should keep before us as our model is very liable to be obliterated by the business of the day. Consequently, in our time, a more regulated and systematic training of conscience is called for.

This can be achieved through regular examination of the state of our conscience. We can put together, in a

kind of scheme for self-examination, the more important duties of the Christian life: something like the Ten
Commandments, only framed in a positive way and
from a strictly Christian point of view. In recent times
many have suggested basing such a scheme on the petitions of the Our Father or on the "great commandment" of love of God and of neighbor. Others suggest
that, especially for young people, conscience can be
trained best by consideration of the nobility of the life
to which Christ calls us and which is possible for us in
him. The heart of the young Christian will leap up with
joy at the thought of the splendor of the Christian life;
he will want to thank God for all the great and noble
deeds and sacrifices that are possible with the aid of
grace. But he will understand too how far off he still is
from the heights of sanctity now unveiled before him.
And this realization, while making him feel small and
humble before God, will also spur him on to struggle
courageously toward the heights, relying on God's
grace.

A detailed examination of the state of one's conscience should be made at least at certain times in the
course of the year: for instance, on recollection days or
at the beginning of Advent and Lent.

PART TWO

CONSIDERATIONS

CHAPTER FIVE

Do Penance

1. "Do penance, for the Kingdom of Heaven is at hand." It was thus that "Jesus began to preach" (Mt 4: 17). And thus already before Jesus did St. John the Baptist proclaim in the desert to those who came out to hear him: "Do penance, for the Kingdom of Heaven is at hand" (Mt 3: 2). To the self-righteous Pharisees and the free-thinking Sadducees he said: "Ye brood of vipers, who hath shewed you to flee from the wrath to come [the wrathful judgment of the coming Messiah]? Bring forth, therefore, fruit worthy of penance." Do not say, he told them, "We have Abraham for our father"— as if family and race and blood were enough. "For now the axe is laid to the root of the trees. Every tree, therefore, that doth not yield good fruit shall be cut down and cast into the fire" (Mt 3: 7–10).

On the occasion when our Lord was told about the Galileans whose blood Pilate had shed as they were offering sacrifice, he appealed most urgently for penance. "Think you," he asked, "that these Galileans were sinners above all the men of Galilee, because they suffered such things? No, I say to you; but unless you shall do penance, you shall all likewise perish. Or those eighteen upon whom the tower fell in Siloe and slew them: think you that they also were debtors above all the men that dwell in Jerusalem? No, I say to you: but except you do penance, you shall all likewise perish" (Lk 13: 1–5). And St. Luke continues: "He spoke also this parable. A certain man had a fig tree planted in his vineyard, and he came seeking fruit on it and found none. And he said to the dresser of the vineyard: 'Behold for these three years I come seeking fruit on this fig tree and I find none. Cut it down, therefore!'" (Lk 13: 6–7).

Penance is commanded for all those who have sinned, even for those who have not sinned grievously. Even the smallest sin calls for penance and can be forgiven only when it is atoned for by penance. We know to what an extent the saints were men of penance, even when they had been guilty of only small sins and imperfections. In St. Aloysius Gonzaga God united a "marvelous innocence of life with equally marvelous penance" and St. Peter of Alcantara was adorned with "the gift of admirable penance and loftiest contemplation" (Collects of their feasts in the old *Roman Missal*). St. Augustine tells us himself in his *Confessions* how he lamented and did penance for the sins and failings of his youth. Penance is the entry door to the heavenly kingdom of sanctifying grace and divine sonship; it is the entry door especially to the heavenly kingdom of Christian perfection, of holy love for God, of the fullness of the gifts of the Holy Spirit and of the truly devout life.

The more we turn away from sin, from all that displeases God in any way or dishonors him or wrongs him, the more we shall be united with him, and the richer will be the life of grace and virtue in us. But that is exactly what penance means: turning away from sin, turning our back on sin: from the first feeling of dissatisfaction with sin up to its complete eradication and the payment of the debt of punishment due to it, and right on to the steadfast determination to embrace always what is good and holy and what honors and glorifies God. Penance is sorrow of soul for the sins we have committed, with the firm resolution to eradicate sin from our lives and to make satisfaction to God for the insults we have offered him in the past. It is really part of the virtue of justice. Its aim is to put an end to the injustice done to God through sin and to reestablish God's right to our service, to the love of our whole heart, and to the activity of our whole being, which is violated by sin. Who would think of doubting that the virtue of penance is a great and sublime virtue!

2. Even those who have never committed mortal sin, who have been guilty only of venial sins and faults of frailty, have need of penance. The saying of St. Ambrose in his treatise on penance is a stern one but, alas, all too true. "It is easier," he wrote, "to find people who preserve their innocence than to find those who do fitting penance for their sins" (*De paenitentia* 2, 10). It so happens that we human creatures, even when we wish to do penance, have much opposition to overcome in ourselves. We do not like to hear about penance and atonement for sin, and, indeed, in actual fact, today in conferences and writings on spiritual things we hear and read but little about penance. Such is the spirit of our time. And yet we all commit sin, we modern people also! And consequently we all need to do penance. Indeed, the more intent we are on striving after perfect union with God and giving him perfect service and living wholly and entirely for him, the more necessary penance is for us.

Even after we have substantially overcome our sinful habits, we still need to go on doing penance. When sin has long since been forgiven by God, it still can and must be bewailed by us, because it remains always something to be regretted, something that ought never to have happened. It has introduced into our relation with God something that should not have been there, something that is out of harmony in a life of true and perfect love of God. And so we can always go on making satisfaction and atonement for the sins of our past that God has already forgiven. We never know how far the punishment for sin is remitted with its guilt, how much temporal punishment for sin we still have to undergo, either here on earth or hereafter in Purgatory. Naturally, then, it is of the greatest moment that, our whole life through, we should, to the best of our ability, always go on atoning and satisfying for our sins; that we should try by a holy zeal for penance ever anew to make reparation to the Lord for our former want of love and self-surrender and loyalty and service.

Penance and satisfaction are necessary for the sins that have already been forgiven us by God. But, alas, aren't we all guilty of sin every day in one way or another? And haven't we, therefore, every day fresh reason for exciting ourselves anew to contrition, atoning for our sins, performing works of penance and reparation, and making up to God for the honor of which we have deprived him?

Yes, indeed, we all need to do penance continually. And there is even a further reason for this. Penance will help us mightily in our struggle toward the heights of the Christian life. An essential element of the interior life is humility. Now, there is scarcely anything else that makes us feel so small and humble before God, the all-holy, who is infinitely pure and noble, than the knowledge and the sorrowful recognition of the fact that we have sinned against him, often and grievously, in thought, word, and deed. The remembrance of our past sins and disloyalty, which God has so mercifully forgiven us, develops in us a sense of gratitude to God. It fills us with gratitude to Christ our Savior, who, by his sufferings and death, won forgiveness for us from the Father. He to whom much has been forgiven loves much (cf. Lk 7: 43). Penance makes us patient and gives us strength to bear our daily cross; it makes us understand better the vanity of the pleasures and good things of this world and helps us to free ourselves interiorly from all earthly ties. Where the spirit of penance is, there also will develop delicacy of conscience and steadfastness against everything that is contrary to God's law and that offends him. And, finally, not the least of the merits of penance is that it produces in the soul a deep, lasting, interior, spiritual joy, which is of great value for the interior life.

3. Do penance! That is, indeed, what we do over and over again in the practice of frequent Confession. Yes, in obedience to the Lord's call, we make up our minds to do penance. We turn away from sin, from even the smallest deliberate sin. Having before our eyes the holiness and goodness of God, we endeavor to understand better what sin means, what even venial sin means. We hate sin with our whole soul, and with our will we turn away from it completely. Our former inclination toward sin is nullified by this new aversion from sin, and any sinful inclination that may still remain is swept away from the soul. And so, as far as our will is concerned, we are no longer the same person we were when we sinned. We have checked our descent, and we are now heading upward. From abhorrence of sin will come sorrow for having treated God so badly; we shall be grieved for having robbed him of honor and for having offended him. Finally, we shall form a definite and firm purpose of amendment for the future: a resolution to avoid sin and the occasions of sin, to make satisfaction and atonement for the sins we have committed, and to make good any damage or injury they may have caused. We shall, too, pray to God fervently for forgiveness and mercy, begging him to take away our sins, to blot them out and forgive them.

With this interior spirit of penance let us come frequently to Confession and receive the sacrament of Penance. Let us come, if possible, every week. Indeed, for religious this is recommended and even prescribed by the Church. And the more pains we take to cultivate such a spirit of penance, the better and the more fruitfully we shall receive the sacrament of Penance.

> *Rebuke me not, O Lord, in thy indignation; nor chastise me in thy wrath. For thy arrows are fastened in me. There is no health in my flesh because of thy wrath; there is no peace for my bones because of my sins. For my iniquities are gone over my head; they weigh like a burden heavy upon me. I will declare my iniquity, and I will think for my sin. Forsake me not, O Lord, my God; do not depart from me.*
>
> —PSALM 38: 1–4, 18, 21

CHAPTER SIX

Sin

I

*If my enemy had reviled me, I would verily have
borne with it. And if he that hated me had spoke
great things against me, I would perhaps have
hidden myself from him. But thou, a man of one
mind, my guide, and my familiar who didst take
sweet meats together with me; in the house of God we
walked with consent. Let death come upon them and
let them go down alive into hell. For there is
wickedness in their dwellings, in the midst of them.*

—PSALM 55: 12—16

1. But thou, my familiar, my friend! Or is he who has
done everything for me not my friend? He took the first
step toward friendship with me when he "emptied himself, taking the form of a servant, being made in the
likeness of men and in habit found as a man" (Phil
2: 7). Could he, the true Son of God, have done more
than descend from the heights of the Godhead to us
men, in order to become our brother, truly man, one of
us? Yes, indeed. "He humbled himself, becoming obedient unto death, even unto the death on the cross"
(Phil 2: 8). That is the second step of the Son of God
toward friendship with us, a step that was exceedingly
painful and distressing and that cost him much. He
"loved me and delivered himself for me" (Gal 2: 20) in
the cruel death of the cross. "Greater love than this no
man hath, that a man lay down his life for his friends"

(Jn 15: 13). And that is exactly what Christ, the Son of God, has done for us. He took a further step toward friendship with us when, in Baptism, he freed us from sin and brought us near to God and raised us up from our lowliness to be sharers of his life, branches of the True Vine, members of his Mystical Body. Could he do more? Yes, as often as we wish it he does still more. In Holy Communion he comes into our hearts every day. He is most anxious to be with us, to pour forth his supernatural life into us, and to fill us with his holiness and his strength and his spirit. Is not this most intimate and holy friendship on his part? But great as it is, it is merely a prelude to that blessed friendship he wants us to enjoy in Heaven: everlasting life with him, in which separation from him will be impossible and in which he will share with us unselfishly and disinterestedly all the good things that are his, his entire inheritance as the Son of God. Thou, my familiar, my friend!

2. And what of us? "He [whom I took for my friend] hath stretched forth his hand to repay" (Ps 55: 20). That is what the sinner does. Insolently and with a terrible want of gratitude he stretches forth his hand against that friend with whom, in Baptism, he entered into a pact of loyalty, and he profanes that friendship. He makes a mockery of the love the Lord showed toward him by becoming man. He disdainfully rejects the heavenly treasures Christ won for him by his life and sufferings and death. He makes worthless and useless, as far as he is concerned, the Savior's countless pains and sacrifices, actions and prayers, bitter sufferings and death. Faithlessly he breaks that baptismal vow he made to renounce Satan and all his pomps. On that occasion, in Baptism, the Lord lifted him up out of his misery, made him his brother, called him, and gave him the power to overcome sin and, with Him and through

Him, to honor the Father in that perfect way in which only those can who are incorporated into Christ through Baptism.

How Christ rejoiced to behold somebody of the same mind as himself, filled with the same hatred of sin and with the same spirit of devotion and love toward the Father: a man after his own heart, his friend and confidant whom he admits to the closest intimacy and to whom he could impart his strength, his secrets, and his very own life! The two together, Christ and his member, would live *one* life, would have *one* outlook, and would pursue *one* ideal and accomplish *one* work: the great work of overcoming evil and worthily and continually glorifying the Father. That is how Christ thought of us; that is what he expected from us.

And what of us? We have sinned in thought, in word, in deed. We have sinned against God, against our neighbor, against ourselves. And not merely once in our life, but often, over and over again. We, who in Baptism were called and dedicated so that together with our Savior we might hate and overcome sin, we have served sin! Instead of being faithful to our vocation and glorifying the Father together with our great High Priest, Christ, we have risen up against him, dishonored him, disregarded his commandments and his holy will and preferred to them our own whims and selfishness. *Mea culpa, mea culpa, mea maxima culpa!* That is what sin is: the basest ingratitude to the Lord, unfaithfulness to the holy covenant we made with him, most unfair treatment of him who has a thousand claims on us and on our life, our thoughts, our desires, and our actions.

In its innermost essence sin is a declaration that "I will not serve"; it is the desire to be as God. My pride wants to have two gods instead of the one true God—namely, God and myself. And that is to do away with

God, to annihilate him, to overthrow him. But God resists pride with all his divine strength, as if from an instinct of self-preservation, from the very necessity of his being. "God resisteth the proud" (James 4: 6). No wonder that Hell exists! No wonder that Satan was cast down from Heaven! Something terrible must surely happen when pride comes up against the indestructible might of the Godhead. Insofar as we in our pride rise against God—and we do this every time we commit sin—we make ourselves enemies of God and companions of Satan. Sin is, indeed, a terrible thing.

Considering all this, it is clear that the first and most important thing for us to do when we go to Confession and in our whole practice of frequent Confession is to excite ourselves with all our strength and energy to contrition for all the sins of our life. We must hate sin above all else and eradicate it entirely from our lives.

> *Have mercy upon me, O God, according to thy great*
> *mercy. And according to the multitude of thy tender*
> *mercies, blot out my iniquity. Wash me yet more from*
> *my iniquity, and cleanse me from my sin. For I know*
> *my iniquity, and my sin is always before me. To thee*
> *only have I sinned, and have done evil before thee.*
> *Thou shalt sprinkle me with hyssop, and I shall be*
> *cleansed, thou shalt wash me and I shall be made*
> *whiter than snow. Turn away thy face from my sins*
> *and blot out all my iniquities. Create a clean heart*
> *in me, O God, and renew a right spirit within my*
> *bowels. Cast me not away from thy face, and take not*
> *thy holy Spirit from me. Restore unto me the joy of thy*
> *salvation, and strengthen me with a perfect spirit.*
> — PSALM 51: 1–4, 7–12

*"Father, I have sinned against Heaven and before
thee. I am not worthy to be called thy son; make me
as one of thy hired servants."*

—LUKE 15: 18–19

1. The younger son in the Gospel parable, being a way-
ward youth, decided to leave his father. "Father," he
said, "give me the portion of substance that falleth to
me" (Lk 15: 12). And he gathered all his possessions
together and went into a far country, a long way from
his father's home.

Such is the man who, through mortal sin, departs
from his Father, God. With what love did God bring
him into existence and endow him with talents and ca-
pabilities! With what love did he lift him up to himself
in Baptism and incorporate him into his own only-
begotten Son, in order to adopt him as his child in
Christ and bestow on him the full love of a father! What
a lordly inheritance he intended for him! Nothing less
than the abundant riches of Christ, "the first-born
amongst many brethren" (Rom 8: 29); Christ's graces
and merits, Christ's salvation and redemption, Christ's
spirit, Christ's life and death, inheritance with Christ in
Heaven.

"Give me the portion of substance that falleth to
me." For what purpose? Because I am not satisfied to be
at home with my father. I am going away. I want a life
that promises more than my father and his friends and
his possessions have to offer.

"And he went abroad into a far country and there
wasted his substance living riotously. And after he had
spent all, there came a mighty famine in that country"
(Lk 15: 13–14). The gifts of grace and sonship of God,

of virtues and moral integrity, the divine gifts of the indwelling of the most holy Trinity in his heart, of the light of faith and of godlike nobility of soul: all these he casts away in exchange for a life of debauchery and sensuality and worldly pleasure.

"And he began to be in want. And he went and cleaved to one of the citizens of that country. And he sent him into his farm to feed swine. And he would fain have filled his belly with the husks the swine did eat; and no man gave unto him" (Lk 15: 14–16). A swineherd, trying to satisfy his hunger from the swine trough! He who was raised up so high by God, nourished with the pure and holy flesh and blood of Christ, inundated with light and strength from the heart of his Father!

"Father, I have sinned against Heaven and before thee" (Lk 15: 18).

2. Sin, mortal sin! Man turns his back on his Father and Creator. He does not want to hear about him anymore; he does not want to listen to him anymore. He withdraws from the love that would make him great and rich forever. He takes as his god some lower instinct, the animal impulse of his lower nature, irrationality.

The sinner withholds from the holy and living God the adoration that is his due. He refuses to trust his infinite love and goodness. He refuses reverence and veneration to the majesty and inviolable holiness of God. He refuses to love him who is supremely worthy of love. He sets up instead a creature, a passion, a momentary pleasure, his own will, himself, as his highest good, as his god, whom he will serve and to whom he will belong.

God bestows on men the most precious of his possessions, the greatest and most sublime gift that can be given in Heaven or on earth: Jesus Christ, true God and true man, who not only is God, worthy of eternal praise, but who also as man possesses in himself all dignity, all nobility, all the greatness of the whole of creation; who, indeed, in himself alone possesses infinitely more dignity and worth than the whole of creation taken together. This precious possession of his the Father presents to us men: the person of Christ, the life of Christ, the grace of Christ, the prayer of Christ, the heart of Christ, the flesh and blood and soul and divinity of Christ: all, everything! And the man who sins? He rejects with indifference this most sublime gift of the Father. What to the Father and to Heaven and earth and to the angels and to men is and must be most sublime, this means nothing to the sinner. He casts it away and has no time for it. Why? A passing pleasure or some gratification or doing his own will means more to him than the Son of God. What terrible disrespect and disdain for God and for Christ!

The Father chose man to be his child, "born of God" (Jn 1: 13), adopted in Jesus Christ into the household and family of God, clothed with the noble garment of sanctifying grace, called to share the blessed life of the Father and the Son and of the Holy Spirit forever hereafter in Heaven. There his soul is destined to drink deep draughts from the wellsprings of truth and peace; and even his now mortal body, endowed with a new life and a perpetually youthful vigor, will be immersed in the pure raptures of the Beatific Vision for all eternity. But all this means nothing to the sinner. He scorns it all and casts it all away. With what result? Only to be torn asunder already in this life by interior anxiety and torment. Only to spend eternity separated from the God of truth and happiness and peace. Only to spend eternity cheated of everything for which his heart ardently and perpetually longs. Only to spend eternity without being able to find anything except what he now seeks in his sin: himself and his own nothingness and desolation. Only to spend eternity with the fallen angels and the dregs of humanity, with the devils, with the slaves of sin and passion. For this it is that the sinner throws away the sonship of God and grace and everlasting bliss. What mad and foolish behavior! What a frightful crime, not only against God and Christ, but also against himself: against his reason, against his own happiness, against his eternal destiny, against his soul, and against his body! "Father, I have sinned."

One excellent means to avoid the danger of sin and to gain strength to resist sin and to overcome it is frequent Confession. If well made, it will preserve us from that tepidity which, slowly but surely, leads to serious sin. It will continually give us new energy to strive after virtue and will bind our will evermore to all that is good, to Christ, to God, and to his holy will.

> *Out of the depths I have cried to thee, O Lord; Lord, hear my voice. Let thy ears be attentive to the voice of my supplication. If thou, O Lord, wilt mark iniquities, Lord, who shall stand it? For with thee there is merciful forgiveness, and by reason of thy law I have waited for thee, O Lord. Because with the Lord there is mercy, and with him plentiful redemption.*
>
> —PSALM 130: 1–4, 7

CHAPTER SEVEN

Venial Sin

I

1. There is mortal sin, namely, sin that by its very nature cuts us off from God and destroys our supernatural life and that, unless repented of and forgiven while we are still here on earth, will separate us from God for eternity. There is also venial sin, namely, sin that by its nature is such that it does not cut us off from God, does not separate us eternally from God, does not condemn us to eternal death and damnation. This is the teaching of the Church, as opposed to the exorbitant exaggerations of Calvin and of Baius (cf. Denzinger, *Echirid. Symb.*, no. 1020). And the Scripture says very truly: "A just man shall fall seven times and shall rise again" (Prov 24: 16). And again: "There is no just man upon earth that doth good and sinneth not" (Eccl 7: 20). St. John writes: "If we say that we have no sin, we deceive ourselves and the truth is not in us" (1 Jn 1: 8). Our own experience confirms this too: for even when we know that we are free from grievous sin, we have to acknowledge humbly every day our sinfulness and implore God to "forgive us our trespasses." And we all must say: "I confess to Almighty God, the Blessed Mary ever virgin, . . . and to all the saints that I have sinned exceedingly in thought, word, and deed."

It may not always be a question of deliberate, fully intended venial sins, committed with full knowledge and consent, such as deliberate neglect of the duties of one's state, squandering of time, sensuality of various kinds, insincerity in speech or behavior, secret hankering after honor, secret vanity, uncharitableness in thought or word or deed. There are also what we call semi-deliberate venial sins, which are committed without full attention or else without full freedom: sins committed through impetuosity or because we are taken off guard. There are, especially, sins of omission. Who is there, no matter how earnestly he is striving to lead a good life, who has not to reproach himself with being wanting in something or other, with having failed to do as much as he could, with not having prayed or made sacrifices or striven to overcome himself as he should have done?

Thus the words of Scripture remain true: "There is no just man upon earth that doth good and sinneth not." Only on one human being was the privilege bestowed of spending a whole lifetime without ever committing the smallest sin of any kind: on Mary, the virgin Mother of God. That, indeed, is the teaching of the Church (Council of Trent, Session VI, ch. 23).

2. Venial sin is also real sin, even if it is essentially different from mortal sin. This latter is such an offense against God that it separates the sinner from him irrevocably and forever; it leads to the eternal loss of God. Venial sin, on the other hand, does not thus cut man off from God; in spite of venial sin he can continue on the way to God and attain to the possession of him. But it is a fatal mistake—though one that is sometimes made today even by Catholics—to regard venial sin and even deliberate venial sin as something harmless, trifling, of no account, as something not forbidden but rather tolerated patiently by God. No, venial sin, though entirely different from mortal sin, is nevertheless sin, that is, a free and deliberate transgression against a command of

God, even if it is a command about something of lesser moment. We tell a lie in regard to some matter that is not in itself very important. By so doing we act against the commandment given by God: "Thou shalt not bear false witness." We know that this commandment exists; we are aware of it at the time: Thou shalt not bear false witness, even in a trivial matter. And, nevertheless, we tell a lie: to avoid some embarrassment or inconvenience. Our own advantage, our own reputation is more important to us at this moment than God's command.

What then do we do when we commit venial sin? We put our wishes, our own interests, our own gratification above God's commands and God's interests. That is what venial sin is: putting God's commands and God's will second to our own interests; dishonoring God, treating God badly, offending the great and holy God and Lord. Venial sin is ungratefulness to him from whom we have received everything. It is disobedience to him whom we should serve wholeheartedly and to whom we should devote our whole lives. Because of our sins God can no longer love us as he could and would if we had kept ourselves free from transgressions. He has to withhold the choicest graces he intended to give us— we force him to act thus. We know that; but we do not care. We are more interested in some momentary gratification of our inordinate desires and our self-love than in God's love and grace. We cannot muster enough love for God and for Christ to enable us to overcome ourselves and magnanimously say no to something. Our love is not perfect; it will not go the whole way; it is wanting in fervor, in fidelity, in tenderness. Such is venial sin.

It is true that venial sin does not take away the supernatural life of the soul, namely, sanctifying grace, by which we are united to God. Nor does it even lessen this.

Sanctifying grace is so pure in itself, so much like a ray of heavenly light in our souls, that it cannot be dimmed or taken away by our venial sins. Nevertheless, venial sin, especially if it is committed frequently and not earnestly repented of and fought against, does great harm to the soul. It represses and weakens the effectiveness of grace and lessens its power. The spiritual energy that formerly impelled the soul continually to acts of the love of God flags and grows languid. The readiness to do each moment what is pleasing to God decreases. The interior ardor of love grows cold. The whole spiritual life, and especially prayer, begins to fail. A thick bank of cloud intervenes between God and the soul at prayer.

Venial sin makes the soul displeasing to God. How could God be pleased with a soul that is casting loving glances at the forbidden? How could he be pleased at vacillation between him and what he must hate? Must not such behavior disgust him? And what will be the result for us? We shall be deprived more and more of the fruitful influence of God's light. Delicacy of conscience, purity of heart, appreciation of God and of what God means to us: all these will decrease. We shall then commit venial sin habitually, without noticing it, and thus sink into a state of tepidity. And this is misery indeed.

How important for us, then, is frequent Confession! For it is one of the very best means we have to counteract and overcome venial sin.

> *O God, who art always ready to have mercy and to forgive: listen, we beseech thee to our earnest prayer and free us and all thy servants from the bonds of sin. Amen.*

II

"As the Father hath loved me, I also have loved you. Abide in my love."

—JOHN 15: 9

Our Savior's request to his Apostles may seem a peculiar one. "Abide in my love": that is, allow me to love you; do not prevent me from loving you and giving you proof of my love. The Savior wants to love us with the love with which the Father has loved him. And how greatly the Father has loved him! Who can understand that everlasting love with which the Father, in an eternal act of generation, has communicated to his Son his whole life and being, his whole divine majesty and blessedness! "All things whatsoever the Father hath are mine" (Jn 16: 15). And when this Son took our human nature in the womb of the Virgin Mary, the Father extended whole and undivided to him as man, to Christ, that same love with which he hath hitherto loved him as his divine Son.

"As the Father hath loved me, I also have loved you." With the fullness of the Spirit that his Father's love pours forth upon him, he takes possession of us also in order to share with us his life, his riches, and his glory. He gives us himself. That is why he drew us so close to him in Baptism. Before our Baptism we were dead, supernaturally. He rescued us from death and made us sharers in his life, just as the Father had made him, the man Christ, a sharer in the divine life. Henceforth Christ wants to be our possession and our property. Everything that is not Christ is too vain and transitory for us. He—with his infinitely precious life, with his power over sin, with his virtues and his holiness—wants to be the whole content of our life. Of ourselves we are very poor, indeed; but now we are infinitely rich in Christ.

"Abide in my love." We commit a deliberate venial sin. That means at least a partial rejection of Christ and of his work of redemption; at least a partial rejection of, and disregard for, the great love shown by the Son of God in becoming man; a partial rejection of his commands, of his wishes, of his interests; a partial rejection of the graces he won for us and consequently of the inheritance destined by him for us in Heaven. What ingratitude, what disrespect and lack of appreciation, what coldness and want of love for Christ are contained in venial sin!

"Abide in my love." Avoid, flee sin, every deliberate venial sin. How pleased our Lord would be if we would allow him to share his life with us wholly and undividedly! Then could he, through us, effectively overcome sin and put Satan to shame and triumph over evil. That would be the triumph of his truth, of his labors, of his sufferings and death, of the Church he founded! But, alas, there are our venial sins!

How pleased Christ would be if he could only pour forth upon us his grace and his divine life without meeting any obstacles! How fruitful his grace would become in us! "He that abideth in me and I in him, the same beareth much fruit" (Jn 15: 5). His grace would then exercise its power in us unhindered. It would entirely subdue nature and all her energies and inclinations and activities and take them into its service. All would be sanctified; all would be done in and with Christ; all would be fruitful for time and for eternity, for us and for the whole Church. How pleased Christ would be if he could live his life in us, if he could reproduce in us and through us, unhindered, his life of prayer, his sentiments of obedience to the Father, his purity, his love of poverty and of suffering, his love for our fellow men! If only he, the Vine, could do all this through us, the branches! How rich and valuable and great and exalted would be our whole life and our deeds and sufferings! But, alas, our venial sins! Must we not, then, do everything to eliminate venial sins from our lives, and especially deliberate, conscious venial sin?

In our practice of frequent Confession we must see to it that the love of Christ grows strong enough in us to make us overcome, through its power, at least deliberate venial sin. The more the love of Christ gains the mastery in our soul, the more securely shall we be protected against venial sin. In trying to free ourselves from venial sin we are laying the necessary foundation for a life in accordance with our baptismal pledge to Christ. By means of frequent Confession, then, let us try to free ourselves from all sin and prepare the way for the perfect love of Christ. The freer we are from sin, the better we shall be able to comply with that entreaty of the Lord: "Abide in my love."

> Lord Jesus, give us the grace by means of the
> sacrament of Penance to respond ever more perfectly
> to that desire of thine that we should abide in thy
> love. Amen.

CHAPTER EIGHT

Overcoming Deliberate Venial Sin

"Be quite sure that this is one of the most important things in the spiritual life and that no spiritual practices, no matter what they are, can lead you to God until you have entirely purified yourself from deliberate venial sin." Thus wrote Father Pergmayr, a German Jesuit of the eighteenth century. And that is the way the saints look on venial sin too. Our whole spiritual and supernatural life will depend on how far we are able to keep ourselves free from venial sin. Hence, we must face the important question: How, by what means, can we overcome venial sin, especially deliberate venial sin?

In our fight to attain complete victory over deliberate venial sin we must follow a certain order. Naturally, we must first of all aim at overcoming those sins that are more serious, either in themselves or on account of particular circumstances (for example, because of their frequency, because of the annoyance they occasion, or because they betray some special weakness). Also we ought first of all to try to eliminate exterior faults; they are easier to discover and also easier to overcome. Then we have to select the right *means* always to overcome our faults.

And here let us put the emphasis on positive means. We drive out darkness by letting in the light. And we should do exactly the same when we want to destroy and cast out from our souls venial sin and its roots: inordinate passions and attachments, bad habits, and so on.

We can do much against venial sin if we try to *prevent* it by constantly and deliberately striving after interior freedom and detachment: trying to free ourselves, even though it costs, from the bonds of created things and of our own selfishness; controlling our senses and our interior dispositions and our passions and our tongue. People may not like the word "mortification," but the thing it signifies is necessary and most important for every earnest Christian. We can prevent venial sin especially by avoiding the occasions of inordinate thoughts and impulses and words and actions.

We can work positively toward the overcoming of venial sin first of all by praying earnestly that God in his mercy may give us the strength and the grace to purify ourselves more and more from venial sin and to preserve ourselves from it. It is, indeed, a work of grace; by ourselves we could never do it. But the grace will be given to us if we pray for it. "Ask and it shall be given you" (Mt 7: 7). So let us pray without ceasing day after day: "Forgive us our trespasses. Lead us not into temptation, but deliver us from evil"; deliver us from the evil of venial sin and preserve us from it.

In practice it is important that we cultivate a right outlook regarding the nature and the significance of venial sin. If we look at things in the light of faith it will be clear to us that, since venial sin insults and offends God, it is a real source of detriment to ourselves and to the common good of our family, our parish or community, even to the Church and to mankind as a whole. The more we come to have a true estimation and evaluation of venial sin, the more likely we are to avoid it and to overcome it gradually. It is of equally great importance that we should have a correct outlook and correct principles regarding the so-called "little things," the various small regulations and minor duties. We persuade ourselves so easily that these rules and regulations are only tiny things, which we can neglect without any disadvantages, which we can disregard without scruple, which we can and ought to treat lightly, about which we need not worry very much. We tell ourselves that God is not so petty and that he does not look too closely at such things.

This is, indeed, a fatal mistake. As if in the spiritual life there could be little things and meaningless regulations! As soon as we shine the light of faith on these little things, they immediately become big and great. For the man who is trying to live by faith, in each and every rule and regulation, even in the most trivial, the will of God manifests itself. Such a person does not see them merely as little things; with the eye of faith he penetrates through the outer shell—some rule or duty, some task or order—and sees the interior kernel: God's will, God's command, God's wish and call. He acquiesces with a wholehearted "Yes, O my God, because you want it this way." Faith makes it easy for him, indeed makes it a necessity for him, to be faithful in small things, even in the smallest things. He does not become petty and crotchety about small things; rather he becomes great and magnanimous about them.

This holds for all circumstances and situations of the Christian life, but it holds especially for religious life. To the religious the voice of God speaks in every prescription of his rule and in every regulation of his superiors. And the more he, in the spirit of faith and of the love of God, holds sacred his vows and his rule and tries to live faithfully according to them, the more will his interior life develop and the better will he be able to overcome his faults and transgressions and venial sins.

Of greater consequence in this striving to overcome venial sins is the proper treatment of the thoughts and impulses of all kinds that come into our minds: impatience, uncharitableness, pride, envy, jealousy, and so on. The best way to behave with regard to these thoughts and impulses is not simply to "put them away," as is frequently said, nor to "fight against them." We should fight against them, by all means. But how? Indirectly. As soon as we are aware of such a thought or impulse within us, we should turn to God, to Christ, with a prayer for help or with an act of trust in his grace and assistance. Or when difficulties or failure or troubles of one kind or another threaten to upset us, we should make an act of resignation to the will of God and to his providence: "Thy will be done"; "All for thy greater glory, O my God." In this way these thoughts and impulses that are an occasion of sin for us can be rendered harmless as soon as they appear. Indeed a temptation to impatience or to anger will be turned into a prayer or into an act of patience or of resignation to God and to his providence. How easily venial sin can be overcome in this way!

If we want to get rid of venial sin it is essential that we seriously set out to develop in our souls a love of God and of Christ. With every increase in this holy love venial sin will lose ground. Love of God compels the soul to surrender itself entirely to him and to his holy will; when that love fills the soul there is no longer any place in it where deliberate disobedience to God can thrive. To the soul that loves God, God and God's interests and God's glory matter above everything. It can refuse God nothing; it can never say no to any desire it recognizes as his or to any disposition he makes, no matter how unimportant it may seem. It is love too that gives the soul the energy to climb to the noble heights of union with God, of life with God and for God. And then there is no longer any room for venial sin. Love, in short, brings all virtues with it. "Charity is patient, is kind, envieth not, dealeth not perversely, is not puffed up, is not ambitious, seeketh not her own, is not provoked to anger, thinketh no evil, believeth all things, hopeth all things, endureth all things" (1 Cor 13: 4–7). Is not that the surest and most direct and best way of overcoming venial sin? "And now there remain faith, hope, and charity, these three; but the greatest of these is charity. Follow after charity" (1 Cor 13: 13; 14: 1). Hence, in the interior life in general, it is of the greatest importance that we should be filled with and guided by the love of God. The more love reigns in us, the more that rather unhealthy and negative way that some people have of striving against venial sin will disappear. All that detailed self-examination and all those almost petty resolutions will no longer be necessary. The soul's outlook will become broader and freer and simpler; it will concern itself only with growing in love. And love will make it extremely sensitive with regard to even the smallest faults; it will be aware of them immediately and will turn back to God again with all the greater loyalty. Love gives the soul the strength to make the sacrifices and renunciations that are necessary if we want to keep our lives free from all deliberate venial sin. Finally, love of God is a powerful enemy of self-love, that ever-present source of most of our faults and failings. "Follow after charity."

Frequent Confession obliges us to set to work earnestly to overcome deliberate venial sin. This must be our attitude and our unshakable determination, if God gives us the grace to practice frequent Confession. And, on the other hand, it is clear that the best proof that our frequent Confessions are well made and fruitful is that they confirm us evermore in our resolve to eradicate venial sin from our lives. Our faithful and laborious striving to overcome deliberate venial sins and failings of every kind is a barometer on which we can read whether and to what degree we are making our frequent Confessions earnestly and fruitfully.

We beseech thee, O God, to purify us and to pour forth thy grace upon us at all times. Amen.

CHAPTER NINE

Sins of Frailty

*And lest the greatness of the revelations should exalt
me, there was given me a sting of my flesh, an angel
of Satan, to buffet me. For which thing, thrice I
besought the Lord that it might depart from me. And
he said to me: "My grace is sufficient for thee, for
power is made perfect in infirmity." Gladly therefore
will I glory in my infirmities, that the power of Christ
may dwell in me.*

— 2 CORINTHIANS 12: 7–9

1. There are many souls so far advanced in virtue that
it is practically impossible for them to commit even the
smallest fully deliberate sin. At the same time they have
to reproach themselves, more or less every day, with certain faults that distress and humiliate them and embar-
rass them before others and irritate those around them.
And this is in spite of their best resolutions, in spite of
all their good will and all the plans they take to free
themselves from these faults.

These are not sins of malice. They are not committed
with open eyes, with full attention of the mind, with full
freedom of the will. They are not the result of an attitude that regards venial sin as a mere trifle, as a thing of
no consequence whatsoever. They are "sins of frailty,"
sins and faults that come from human weakness and
that ultimately are the result of original sin. It is true
that in themselves these faults, objectively considered,

are transgressions of God's commands, for example, the thoughtless taking of God's name. But there is no real sin on the part of the person who thus, without reflecting, calls on God's name. The conditions required for sin are not present; the knowledge, the advertency of mind, and the full and free consent of the will are either entirely wanting (as in the example of the thoughtless taking of God's name), or at any rate consent is so imperfect and limited that there is no real sin at all.

2. Faults of frailty occur either through lack of advertency or on account of weakness of will. Faults of frailty due to *lack of advertency* are those faults that come from thoughtlessness, impetuosity, want of reflection: because we are taken unawares, surprised, thrown into confusion momentarily. They are not the results of a deliberately adopted attitude of mind; on the contrary, they are quite opposed to our permanent dispositions and are, so to speak, external and accidental to us. They are the result of some particular transitory situation: momentary, passing sins rather than sins that arise from our real inclinations. In spite of the best intentions in the world we fall into many such sins. Provided the thoughtlessness that causes them is not in itself in any way culpable, there is no real sin in faults of frailty of this kind. Nevertheless, we do not feel unconcerned and indifferent about them. The moment we become aware, for instance, that in a hasty moment we have said something we ought not to have said, we are sorry for it, and we resolve anew to be more careful on similar occasions in the future. If we have given offense to somebody, we try to make up for it as best we can.

Faults of frailty that come from a certain *weakness of will* are somewhat different. When a sudden movement of impatience or of anger arises in us, very often we are conscious immediately that this is not right. But our will lets itself be carried along automatically, by force of instinct. It refuses, because it is too weak, to fight sufficiently against an impulse, for example, of sensuality or curiosity, of bitterness or jealousy or irritability, against the tendency to be critical and discontented, against the inordinate desire to put oneself in the limelight and to be esteemed and considered interesting and important. And so on.

Here on earth we can never fully eliminate faults of frailty or make them impossible. The Church teaches us so expressly (Council of Trent, Session VI, ch. 23), and St. James tells us that "in many things we all offend" (James 3: 2). Even the saints frankly acknowledge that they were sinners. Even in them we see that here on earth men can never attain that complete and absolute perfection which excludes all waverings and faults.

It is a consolation for us to know, however, that these sins and faults of frailty, so far from doing us harm, can, on the contrary, if properly managed, lead us to God and be, as it were, a grace for us. Let us remember that the fervor of our spiritual life is measured, not by the number of our sins and faults, but by the degree of our love of God, of our charity. Growth in love counts for much more than occasional sins of frailty—which, besides, need not hinder growth in love but, rather, can even promote it. For we can benefit by our daily faults of frailty in three ways. (a) Through these faults we discover and come to see vividly our own limitations, our insufficiency, our failure. This is a very good remedy against self-complacency, self-conceit, self-satisfaction, self-righteousness; it is the road to humility. (b) With the humble recognition of our own weakness and insufficiency goes the knowledge that we must expect nothing from ourselves but everything, even the greatest things, from God. "Power [the power of Christ: grace] is made perfect in infirmity [in the infirmity of men]. Gladly therefore will I glory in my infirmities, that the power of Christ may dwell in me. . . . For when I am weak, then am I powerful" (2 Cor 12: 9–10). Our infirmity, if we humbly resign ourselves to it, gives us straightaway a claim on God's grace. And thus our very faults make us trust more in God. (c) Our faults of frailty can again and again in the course of the day be the means of positively leading us to God and to Christ. They can become occasions on which we can raise our hearts to God and make an ejaculation: expressing contrition, asking him for help, thanking him for his aid in the past, assuring him of our loyalty and resignation. And so, if we only react properly to these faults, they can be the means of keeping our souls in constant contact with God; they can help us to be more prayerful and more closely united to God.

It would, of course, be a great mistake if, as a matter of principle, we regarded these faults of frailty as insignificant trifles that can be neglected or ignored. No, these faults are displeasing to the all-holy God, and therefore we cannot be indifferent about them. On the contrary, we must sincerely endeavor to get them under control and, at the very least, to lessen their number. But how? First of all by recognizing their positive value and using them to bring us nearer to God. With the eye of faith we can see our weaknesses as a cross that God has laid upon us for our whole lives. Let us accept this cross; let us take it up and bear it patiently for love of God. Let us humble ourselves: before God and in our own eyes and before others who may be the witnesses of our failures. Let us make our failures occasions for raising our hearts to the Lord and asking him to help us to stand steadfast; let us make them occasions for committing ourselves to his keeping with the fullest trust. The important thing always is love for God. When love for God is the motive force of our lives, then inordinate self-love—the deepest root and the source of almost all our faults and weaknesses—is continually losing its power and its influence. Instead, with love of God and of Christ, there grows in us the love of our neighbor and the strength to be patient and forgiving, to put up with difficulties and to overcome ourselves. Our interior detachment from earthly pleasures and goods and interests, from the things and the people of this world, increases. We develop a Christlike single-mindedness that looks only to God and to his glory and will and interests and that never yields weakly to human respect.

It is the ardor of love that dries up the sources both of deliberate venial sin and of faults of frailty. It is the quickest and the surest way to success in checking and decreasing these faults. It often happens that certain of our weaknesses and human failings involve us in various embarrassments before our companions. We can well atone for such faults by humbly accepting such consequences of our failure. Thus we can deal with our various faults of frailty in such a way that they will become for us a road to holiness and virtue and self-surrender to God. Finally, let us try to track down the deeper sources of our faults of frailty and impetuosity. These sources lie in our lack of control over our senses and our emotions and in the weakness of our will. Nothing can be effected here without purposeful effort on our part, without prayer and self-denial, and without God's saving grace, that is, without a high degree of sanctifying grace and of the theological virtues of faith, hope, and charity that are infused into the soul along with it.

3. As we make progress in the interior life we shall gradually arrive at the state in which we commit and have to confess practically no other sins except sins of frailty. And it is precisely now that frequent Confession must face the test. The person who practices frequent Confession has a duty to this holy sacrament and to himself and to the Church to get to work in real earnest at checking his faults of frailty. Not without truth has it been said that "pious people" are the worst enemies of Christianity and of Christ and of the Church: because they do not live up to their religion and because in spite of frequent Confession and Holy Communion they give scandal by their lack of self-control, by their failure in charity, by their moodiness, their touchiness, and so on. They fail entirely in practice to give proof in their lives of that power which our faith and our holy sacraments possess: the power to transform us, to fashion us into new creatures who in all things reproduce and display the spirit and outlook of Christ.

The penitent who is not really in earnest about getting his daily faults of frailty and impetuosity under control is only misusing frequent Confession. If frequent Confession is going to be effective and fruitful with regard to these faults, we must proceed with set purpose according to a certain plan. We must take first of all as matter for our Confessions those faults that appear outwardly, that get on other people's nerves, that give scandal, that bring piety into bad repute. And of set purpose too we must observe the principle: a little, but well done. We must take a few, or even just one, of these faults, making sure that our contrition is sincere and that our purpose of amendment is definite and concrete and directed right at the deepest roots of the fault in question. It is obvious, of course, too that we must pray earnestly for the grace to acquire more and more fully the mastery over this and that fault, assiduously persevering in making it the matter of our Confession for weeks or even for months at a time, if necessary. The sacrament of Penance itself increases sanctifying grace in our souls and brings in its train a rich abundance of actual graces. The spiritual energy of the new supernatural man in us is thus intensified, and the whole activity of our instincts and emotions and will is subjected to the invigorating influence of grace. In this way frequent Confession acquires an immense importance for the development and advancement of our spiritual life. It becomes, in truth, a great help and grace to the earnestly striving Christian.

> *Almighty and eternal God, look down graciously on our weakness and stretch forth the right hand of thy majesty to protect us, through Christ our Lord. Amen.*

CHAPTER TEN

The Perfect Life

1. Our times are times of crisis. Men fear and lament; they feel uncertain and disturbed. The old principles are no longer accepted; new theories are propounded about everything: about the state, politics, economics, social life, law, morality; about the whole Christian life and even about the Church and the Faith. Proposals of all kinds are made and the most diverse means are recommended as remedies for the ills of the world. Today, therefore, it is more necessary than ever for us to open our hearts to the call of God, who alone can show us the way to deliverance and safety, and to heed his voice telling us: "Be renewed in the spirit of your minds" (Eph 4: 23).

The fundamental evil that afflicts our times and from which we all suffer is that the interior life of men, even of Christians, has grown weak. The remedy is not that we fall in with the principles of the world or with what is called "public opinion," that we adopt the tendencies and outlook of the passing moment, but rather that we withdraw into ourselves and try to become aware of the supernatural powers with which God has endowed us and see to it that these develop fully: until we think and live in a truly Christian way. What our times need is new men, really Christian men; true, interior, perfect Christians who with all their strength try to answer the call of the Lord: "Be ye perfect, as also your heavenly Father is perfect" (Mt 5: 48). This is, indeed, a high ideal!

Our Lord explained it in detail in the Sermon on the Mount. "Unless your justice abound more than that of the Scribes and Pharisees, you shall not enter into the Kingdom of Heaven" (Mt 5: 20). Then six times in succession he contrasts the new Christian perfection with that of former times: "It was said to them of old. . . . But I say to you. . . ." The Kingdom of Heaven, Christian perfection, consists not in words, not in saying "Lord, Lord," but in deeds that give proof of its worth; in the fact that we are poor in spirit and meek, that we hunger and thirst after justice, that we are peaceful and forgiving, that we are ready to sacrifice the things that are dearest to us if they become for us a cause of sin, that we love our enemies and wish them well and do good to them, that we treat our brethren in all things as they have a right to expect to be treated by fellow Christians (see Mt 5: 1–42).

The Sermon on the Mount is not just a piece of well-meant advice intended for the few, for an *élite*. Rather, it is a law that holds for each and every one of us. We must begin to take that sermon seriously. It often requires courage to be different from others, not to follow the crowd, to be misunderstood, misrepresented, judged wrongly, condemned, ridiculed. But Christ bids us take courage: "Enter ye in at the narrow gate: for wide is the gate and broad is the way that leadeth to destruction, and many there are who go in thereat. How narrow is the gate and strait is the way that leadeth to life: and few there are that find it!" (Mt 7: 13–14). "Beware of false prophets, who come to you in the clothing of sheep, but inwardly they are ravening wolves. By their fruits you shall know them. . . . A good tree cannot bring forth evil fruit. . . . Every tree that bringeth not forth good fruit shall be cut down and shall be cast into the fire" (Mt 7: 15–19). And Christ is terribly in earnest in this sermon: "Everyone that heareth these my words and doth them not shall be like a foolish man that built his house upon the sand. And the rain fell and the floods came and the winds blew: and they beat upon that house. And it fell: and great was the fall thereof" (Mt 7: 26–27). On the other hand, he who hears his words and follows them is like "a wise man that built his house upon a rock." The rains and floods and winds may come, but it will not fall because there it is "founded on a rock" (Mt 7: 24–25).

The Lord demands much, it is true. Sometimes he asks even the heroic. How can we give him what he asks? We must remember that in living according to the Sermon on the Mount, as in so many other things, there are different degrees. We must distinguish between beginning, making progress, and attaining perfection. The true Christian keeps on striving indefatigably to live according to the high ideals of the Sermon on the Mount. Without ceasing, he fights on with a holy dissatisfaction in his heart. For we can never sit back and say: I have attained my goal. Rather, we must with St. Paul "press toward the mark" and try to reach it. "I do not count myself to have apprehended. But one thing I do. Forgetting the things that are behind and stretching forth myself to those that are before, I press toward the mark, to the prize of the supernal vocation of God in Christ Jesus" (Phil 3: 13–14).

2. What is Christian perfection? It is not something apart from the other duties of a Christian nor does it go beyond them. It is not a special duty. It is merely the full, entire, and assiduous performance of all our duties: the full carrying-out of all our obligations, as members of the Church and as citizens of the State, as men and as Christians, at home and in public, in the sphere of the natural and the supernatural. In short:

Christian perfection is made up of the sum total of all our duties.

The perfect life, however, does not consist in a multitude of pious exercises, prayers, and devotions, or in merely exterior practices, or in the performance of exterior acts of sacrifice and of virtue, or even in difficult works of self-denial and penance. Perfection is an interior thing. It is a disposition, an interior attitude. It is, especially, the attitude of perfect love for God, the fulfillment of the great commandment "Thou shalt love the Lord thy God with thy whole heart and with thy whole soul and with thy whole mind" (Mt 22: 37). We are perfect in the measure in which we have attained union with God and become like him. But this comes about through charity, through love; it is love that unites us to God and makes us like unto him. "He who is joined to the Lord is one spirit" (1 Cor 6: 17): like two flames that join together and fuse into one.

The measure of our perfection is our love, our charity. Now, everyone who is in the state of sanctifying grace—that is, everyone who keeps God's Commandments and avoids mortal sin—possesses charity. Is he then perfect? No; we are in the full sense perfect only from the moment when love or charity is so strong and effective in us that it lifts us above every, or almost every, deliberate unfaithfulness, transgression, venial sin and preserves us from all such. Indeed, we are really perfect only when the love of God makes us and keeps us so strong and so much on the alert that we avoid as much as possible even sins and faults of frailty and impetuosity, or at least try to lessen their number and variety. But this is only one side of the perfect life, the negative side. Perfection really shows itself in all its greatness and fullness in its positive side. The perfect man does all good, that is, he does all and everything that is commanded by

God and that he could not omit without sinning, without offending God. Moreover, he goes beyond that which is commanded by God, what is of obligation, and does, as far as he can, much more than is commanded, much more than what he could not omit or do otherwise without sinning. He does not merely do what is good and right; he endeavors also to do the better thing, that which gives greater glory to God, advances his interests more, and is more pleasing to him. That is love at its best, in its perfection. It makes us avoid not merely everything that displeases God but also everything that pleases him less; and it impels us to do what pleases him more and what honors and glorifies him more. Perfection means doing all good and doing it perfectly, both interiorly and exteriorly. Doing it perfectly interiorly, that is to say, with perfect dispositions: from the motive of the love of God, for his sake, to honor him and to do his holy will. And doing it perfectly exteriorly, that is, with complete fidelity, punctuality, attention, and care. And all this not just for a few days or a few months but continually, day after day and month after month, during the whole of life, unweariedly, ever trying anew to achieve greater perfection and greater purity of soul and greater holiness

Progress toward Christian perfection and the attainment of it is the result not so much of our own efforts as, rather, of the action of grace in us. It is God himself who labors in us to raise us up to perfect union with him. For this purpose he takes hammer and chisel in hand and sets to work on our souls to make them all pure and beautiful and worthy of himself. We must pass through darkness and trials, both spiritual and temporal, so numerous and so profound "that neither does human knowledge suffice for the understanding of them, nor experience for the description of them" (St.

John of the Cross, *Ascent of Mount Carmel,* Prologue). Our object is a complete victory over self-love, sensuality, sloth, and impatience, over the impulses of nature and over our purely natural interests, over everything that is an obstacle to the spirit of faith, of trust in God, and of wholehearted love of him. And this is not achieved without much affliction and hardship and suffering, both interior and exterior, without great and painful aridity and darkness and anguish of soul, even to the extent of feeling rejected and abandoned by God himself. Only when the soul has endured this painful "purification" is it ready for perfect union with God. Then God gives himself to the soul in all his wonderful splendor and transforms it. God and the soul become one: just like glass and the sunshine that streams through it, like fuel and the fire that is consuming it.

3. Christian perfection is life, true life, the very fullest life: a possession infinitely exalted in comparison with any natural endowment, in comparison with earth and anything earthly life has to offer us.

Christian perfection is fullness. It is the full blossoming of love. And with love all the Christian virtues attain their development; by it they are linked together firmly, and their common strength and effectiveness are increased. Only under the influence of love can the activity of the perfect soul be truly what it should be.

Finally, Christian perfection is the most sublime glorification of God. It is a continual holy song of praise of God—of his goodness, his power, his love, his purity, his holiness. It is a continual and perfect act of homage to his commandments, to his holy will, to his every wish, to every inspiration of his grace. It is a wholehearted "Yea, Father" to whatever he demands or gives or takes. "Yea, Father: for so it hath seemed good in thy sight" (Mt 11: 26).

What our time needs above all is fully and really perfect Christians, religious and lay people who take the Sermon on the Mount seriously. Why is it that so many priests and religious and pious people in the world live such purely natural lives? Why is it that they become angry if anybody finds fault with them or says an unfriendly word to them, that they are so concerned about what others think of them, that they are so fond of their own comfort and seek so much that which flatters their self-love? The reason is chiefly that, through venial sin and frequent imperfections, they hinder or limit the working of the Holy Spirt in their souls, but also that they do not go to sufficient trouble to free themselves from venial sin and its roots. For the first step on the road to perfection is the overcoming of venial sin.

Here let us recognize, as far as frequent Confession is concerned, that this practice has as its precise aim the overcoming of venial sin. Is it just by chance that the Church makes frequent or even weekly Confession obligatory for all those who are specially bound to strive after Christian perfection: for priests, seminarians, religious? (See *Code of Canon Law*, 1917, canons 125, 595, 1367.) No; in the mind of the Church frequent Confession is a particularly effective means toward Christian perfection. Pope Pius XII recommended highly the practice of frequent Confession as a way of "a constant and speedy advancement in the path of virtue." "By this means," he wrote, "bad habits are uprooted, spiritual negligence and apathy are prevented, the conscience is purified and the will strengthened" (*Mystici Corporis*, no. 87). Hence, frequent Confession is a particularly valuable means at our disposal in the struggle to attain the goal that is set before us. Let us esteem it as it deserves and take pains to make our Confession well. And let us, by our earnest striving after Christian perfection in our daily lives, try to prove to all around us the power of frequent Confession.

> *O Lord, thou hast, through the grace of the Holy Spirit, poured forth into the hearts of thy faithful the gifts of love. Grant unto us that we love thee with all our strength and accomplish with the fullness of love what is well pleasing to thee. Amen.*

CHAPTER ELEVEN

Imperfections

Follow after charity.

— 1 CORINTHIANS 14: 1

1. The Gospel sets a high ideal before us: "It becometh us to fulfill all justice" (Mt 3: 15). Our Lord recommended a life of celibacy "for the Kingdom of Heaven" (Mt 19: 12). To the rich young man he said: "If thou wilt be perfect, go sell what thou hast and give to the poor and come follow me" (Mt 19: 21). In the Sermon on the Mount he declared: "I say to you not to resist evil: but if one strike thee on the right cheek, turn to him also the other. And if a man will contend with thee in judgment and take away thy coat, let thy cloak also unto him. And whosoever will force thee one mile, go with him other two. Give to him that asketh of thee: and from him that would borrow of thee turn not away" (Mt 5: 39–42). To the man who wished to follow him but who would first go and bury his father he said: "Let the dead bury their dead: but go thou and preach the Kingdom of God" (Lk 9: 60). "All things whatsoever you would that men should do to you, do you also to them" (Mt 7: 12). And what our Lord taught, that he put into practice himself in the most perfect way possible.

It is not sufficient that we avoid sin and try to eliminate it from our lives. We must also do good and do it perfectly. Our daily life is made up of a great number of actions, thoughts, desires, and works that are either good or, in themselves, morally indifferent. Writing a letter, reading an unobjectionable book, studying, resting after doing work, going to meals and taking the food that is necessary for us, availing ourselves of an opportunity to go for a walk or have some recreation—these are all things that in themselves are indifferent. They are in no way sinful; they are morally unobjectionable. If we do them with a right intention, they are good actions.

We do, indeed, do much good in our lives. But often we do not do it *as well as*, under the given circumstances, we could. And often too we do not do *all* the good that we could do under the circumstances. In other words, we could do more good; and we could do that which we do better and more perfectly. We fulfill that to which we are bound before God and in conscience, that which God commands us to do; and thus we avoid sin. But it would please God better and give him more honor and glory if we did still more good and if we did the good that we do in a still more perfect way. God would prefer that, though he does not strictly oblige us to it. We could, for instance, pray more, pray oftener, and pray better. We could exercise more self-control, overcome ourselves more, make more sacrifices. We could deny ourselves various little pleasures, insofar as it is allowed us to do so. We could become more detached from worldly and sensual things. We could give up many practices and activities and relationships in which something blameworthy all too easily enters. We could do the good that we do with more fervor and perseverance and determination, more cheerfully and devotedly. We could love our neighbor, approach him in a more friendly and warm-hearted manner, and show ourselves ready to help him even beyond that which the law of charity strictly and absolutely requires. Religious could observe their holy vows better and more faithfully. We are acting perfectly *quantitatively* when we do all the good that in our circumstances is possible, in other words, when we make use of every opportunity to do good that presents itself, including all the little opportunities that come our way daily and hourly. But perfection demands in addition that *qualitatively* we act always as well as possible in both big things and little things; that in all our actions our interior intentions should be as pure as possible and that the exterior execution should be carried out at the right moment and in the right way. If we have to admit that some good actions of ours could have been done better, as regards either the interior motive or the external performance, it is still true of course that we have acted well and rightly. We have done what God commanded; we have not transgressed God's law; we have not sinned. But we could have acted better. In other words, our action was morally good but imperfect, not perfect.

2. How are we to regard such imperfect conduct? We do something good, or at least morally indifferent; it is not bad, it is not sinful. What we do, therefore, is in itself not a sin; it is not a transgression of any command of God. Still, often enough, such an action is not faultless; it is rendered imperfect by the motive from which it proceeds. This motive may be some inordinate attachment: to a person, to a particular kind of work, to one's health, to money or possessions. Or it may be a certain sensuality, a certain reserve in making sacrifices, a desire for one's own comfort, some form of inordinate self-seeking—ultimately, some wrong tendency in the will. On account of this sinful tendency in the will from which they originate, imperfections can be made

matter for Confession. Even though imperfections are not themselves sins, they can have very serious effects on the progress and development of the interior life. An imperfection always means the disregard of the wishes and, to put it in a human way, the expectations of God, for the sake of some like or dislike of our own. God does not command, he only recommends, that I do a certain thing or do it in a certain way. But I pay no heed to his wishes because I prefer something else that pleases me better. I drink a glass of water, for instance, to quench my thirst. The determining motive in my drinking is my desire to quench my thirst. I forget God completely; I am concerned only with myself and my own satisfaction. I put myself and my own needs in the first place, before God. Do I commit a sin? No, I do not. Is my action imperfect? Could it not be better, more perfect? Yes, it could be better, and it should be.

An imperfection means that we seek ourselves rather than God's honor and this in good or morally indifferent actions and where there is no question of a definite offense against God. It means disorder, an inversion of right order; for right order demands that God should be put in the first place and myself second. Consequently, an imperfection always means an opportunity of doing good wasted; and habitual imperfection means a diminution of the value of our whole life, made up as it is of good and morally indifferent actions. Through our imperfections we deprive ourselves of many graces and rob ourselves of moral force and energy. The development of our whole religious life is delayed and hindered. Our growth is retarded, and we remain spiritual dwarfs, little stunted, misshapen creatures. We were given five talents to trade with, but our profits are the same as if we had been given only two. How can God be satisfied with us?

It is, therefore, a matter of importance for us that we rise above this imperfect way of acting, which can show itself in so many ways. And how can we do this? By instilling into ourselves a deep appreciation of the holiness and sublimity of the things of the supernatural life and a high esteem of what is "better," of what is perfect. And, ultimately, that means understanding that glorifying and praising God is the greatest thing we can do. By means of this high esteem for what is perfect and this zeal for the honor of God we shall soon succeed in reaching a stage when we no longer act thoughtlessly from purely human and natural motives, as we all are so wont to do. We shall also rise above the motive of the fear of God's punishment and even above the motive of the hope of Heaven, that is to say, above the motive of imperfect love. We shall strive particularly to cultivate more and more perfect love for God and for Christ.

This does not mean that we have to suppress entirely all our good natural impulses and motives. It means that, insofar as they are good and noble, we have to subject them to, and make them serve, the great motive of perfect love. They all have to be elevated by it. God and his honor, his will, his wishes, his interests—these must come first with us. In all and through all we must press forward with a strong spirit of faith and a heart full of love for him. The more we allow ourselves to be guided and determined by the perfect love of God, the more we shall be able to purify ourselves from imperfections and to rise to a perfect life and give perfect glory to God in every way. For the full meaning of the Christian life is realized only in the carrying out of "the greatest and the first commandment": "Thou shalt love the Lord thy God with thy whole heart and with thy whole soul and with thy whole mind" (Mt 22: 37).

3. Can imperfections be matter for Confession? In

themselves, no, because an imperfect action is not, in itself, a sin. A prayer said with involuntary distractions and lack of attention is not a sin; on the contrary, insofar as there is a genuine desire to pray, it is a good prayer and pleasing to God, as long as the lack of attention is not deliberate. Nevertheless, the causes that are responsible for our imperfections can be matter for Confession. These causes are, for instance, an inordinate attachment to our own interests or to certain creatures, works, or pursuits; love of ease, reluctance to make sacrifices, sensuality, a frivolous disposition; in every case, some disordered inclination of the will.

Considering these causes of our imperfections and considering too the nature and the pernicious effects of imperfections, it is clearly important that we set to work seriously to do something about them. In our examination of conscience and in our accusation in Confession let us search out the sources and causes of our imperfect actions. Let us deliberately formulate our purposes of amendment in a positive way: "I will, to the best of my knowledge and ability, do all the good that is possible for me in my circumstances; I will do it in the way that gives more honor to God and to my Savior, in the way that is more pleasing to God, with great fervor and great fidelity. The good that I do, I will do from the motive of perfect love, so that all other good natural motives and all supernatural but still imperfect motives will be supported and animated by this motive of perfect love." When we go to work in this positive manner, we strike a powerful blow at the causes of our imperfect behavior, and we are well on the road to attaining the object after which we are striving. Love, the motive of love and the subordination of all other motives to the motive of love, will prove decisive and bring us victory. It is clear, of course, that to carry out this program we need the help of great and powerful graces. We must ask God for them in assiduous and humble prayer.

The confessor can be and should be a great help to us here. It behooves him to do everything he can to help us attain the heights of the perfect life and do the good that we do fully and perfectly.

Let us, then, use well the great means we have in frequent Confession so that, with the assistance of God's grace, our daily lives may become a true and full-sounding hymn of glory to the Father and the Son and the Holy Spirit, unspoiled by the discord of imperfections.

> *Enlarge my heart with thy love, O Lord, that I may have an interior knowledge of how sweet it is to love and to be consumed by love and to revel in love. Let me be possessed by love; let me rise above myself in an ecstasy of love. Let me sing the hymn of love. Let me follow thee, my Beloved, on high. Let my soul be lost in thy praise, singing aloud to thee in love. Let me love myself only for thee, and let me love in thee all that truly love thee.*
>
> *Imitation of Christ*, BK. 3, CH. 5

CHAPTER TWELVE

Self-Love

1. "Two different kinds of love have given origin to two cities, a heavenly city and an earthly one," writes St. Augustine. "Self-love, even unto contempt of God, gave origin to the earthly one; love of God, even unto contempt of self, gave origin to the heavenly one" (*De civ. Dei*, 14.28). On these two kinds of love, self-love and love of God, the whole life and fate of each one of us and of all mankind turns.

There is good, right, well-ordered self-love; and there is a wrong, disordered, and sinful self-love.

Well-ordered self-love is set before us as the norm for the love of our neighbor. "Thou shalt love thy neighbor as thyself" (Mt 19: 19). And St. Paul writes: "No man ever hated his own flesh [that is, himself], but nourisheth and cherisheth it, as also Christ does the Church" (Eph 5: 29). The Church upholds well-ordered self-love and she has condemned more than once the view that it is sinful to act from the sole motive of one's own salvation. She declares that it is impossible for us always and constantly to strive after perfection, virtue, and salvation for God's sake alone, to the exclusion of every consideration of our own desire for happiness (cf. Denzinger, *Enchirid. Symb.*, nos. 1330ff., 1345). No, we may love ourselves and wish well to ourselves. Indeed, we must love ourselves—our very nature demands that we do so; the desire for happiness is innate in us. May we not, should we not love God, our neighbor, virtue, and eternal salvation for the reason also that they are "good" for us: because in them our natural desire for happiness is satisfied and our deepest longings fulfilled? Yes, this rightly ordered love of ourselves is the natural prerequisite and foundation for our love of God. For, according to St. Bernard: "Man first loves himself for his own sake. Then he sees that he himself alone is not enough, and he begins to love God, not for God's sake but for his own. Then he gets to understand God better and begins to love God for God's sake and not for his own" (*De dilig. Deo,* 15.39).

We may quite lawfully desire natural gifts for ourselves: talents, knowledge, strength of character, a resolute will, all noble human qualities. We may also lawfully love our body and be solicitous for it; always, however, preserving a right order: putting the care of our soul first and making sure that it is master over the body, that it grows in virtue, draws near to God, and strives after eternal salvation. Our self-love is perfectly ordered if we love ourselves for God's sake; that is, if we love ourselves as creatures, as children of God, as the instruments of his glory, called to serve him, to work for him, to suffer for him, to receive and use his gifts and graces, to do his adorable will in all things.

Well-ordered self-love becomes a holy hatred of self. In us all, indeed, there are many things worthy of hatred: the sins that we commit, our inclination to sin, and our sloth in doing good. We show hatred for ourselves by punishing ourselves for the sins we have committed, by counteracting our inclination to evil with self-denial and mortification, by endeavoring with all our strength to do good. In particular, we show hatred for our body when we bring it under control and make it submit to the law of the spirit, to reason, and to the Commandments and norms of the Gospel. Self-hatred of this kind is a holy duty for us.

"If any man come to me and hate not . . . his own life, he cannot be my disciple" (Lk 14: 26). "If any man will come after me, let him deny himself" (Mt 16: 24). This hatred of self is really a holy self-love. And it is a necessary foundation of true and strong love of God. "In order to love God perfectly, we must hate ourselves perfectly," says a spiritual writer. And that is the view of the saints too. For St. John of the Cross this holy self-hatred, with which he declared war on himself as his own worst enemy, was the starting point for his great and extraordinary holiness. "I chastise my body and bring it into subjection" (1 Cor 9: 27). Would that we also were filled with this holy hatred against ourselves and especially our flesh and its inordinate claims!

2. Inordinate self-love is called also selfishness, or self-seeking. It is the deepest and the ultimate root of all the sins and faults in our lives. Already in the Garden of Eden self-seeking caused sin. And the whole catalogue of men's crimes, of their wars and dissensions and hatreds, from the beginning right up to the present day, is really nothing else but the continual manifestation of the self-seeking and self-love that is so deeply seated in the human heart. Self-love is the root of all evil passions; it causes great suffering to mankind: in the community, in the family, in the hearts of individuals.

We Christians too fall victims to self-love, even we who are trying hard to lead a life that is worthy of God and of Christ. Self-love makes us show more indulgence and benevolence to ourselves than we deserve, with the result that God and our neighbor are deprived of the love that we owe them.

Very often self-love puts the things of the body—bodily health, temporal prosperity, comfort and ease, bodily strength or beauty—above the good of the soul and makes us unduly concerned about these things, which are, after all, of secondary importance.

Even in spiritual things self-love makes us seek excessively after progress in virtue and freedom from every fault and weakness, out of a secret ambition and vanity and pride. It causes our souls to be disturbed and dissatisfied and impatient when our prayer and our spiritual exercises are not going as we wish them to go, when we are troubled with distractions and so forth and cannot pray as well as we should like to and as we thought we could.

In our behavior toward those around us, especially, self-love shows itself. It makes us touchy and short-tempered, sharp, conceited, censorious; it makes us cold, unfeeling, unfriendly, envious, unfair in judgment and in speech, lacking in respect for others; it takes away that interior peace that is the very soul of the spiritual life. It produces in us an exaggerated sense of our own importance and thus destroys humility. It creates a jealous, distrustful disposition and makes us day by day more irritable and touchy and more incapable of practicing charity and causes us to lead a very superficial and distracted life, without any deep or genuine attention to the things of God. It makes us consider ourselves better than others, even in matters of piety; it makes us close our eyes to their good points, see only their shortcomings and defects, and ascribe to them evil intentions that they never had.

In the life of the community, of the family, of the parish, of the monastery or convent, self-love inclines people to go their own way as far as possible, to look for dispensations from the common regime, and, at the same time, to be stricter in certain other things than the law or the common practice demands. Self-love makes us seek always what is special and peculiar; it makes us want to be different, to attract attention, to be in command, to be considered important. It very likely makes us disobedient, inclined to criticize, to be dissatisfied, to be wanting in charity toward our superiors and equals.

Self-love is the source of much interior disturbance, disquiet, fear, and disillusionment. It often gives rise to a multitude of "good resolutions" and plans that never let the soul rest and deprive it of all interior peace. It is the deep and ultimate cause of all our sins and faults and unfaithfulness.

The world, the flesh, and the devil can harm us only when they find within us an enemy with whom they can form an alliance. Self-love is the enemy of God. The self-loving man is concerned only about himself; he loves himself and not God. Self-love is the declared opponent of God and of the holy love of God. And because it is the enemy of the love of God, it is also the enemy of the Christian love of our neighbor. Love, charity, St. Paul tells us, true charity "is kind, envieth not, seeketh not her own" (1 Cor 13: 4–5).

Indeed, for that matter, self-love is the enemy of all noble human qualities and of all genuine affection. It makes us insincere, unprincipled, two-faced, moody, dissembling, mean; and it is often the source from which hysterical behavior originates. "Genuine fraternal charity lives with a thousand souls; self-love lives with only one soul, and that is narrow, small and wretched," says a recent writer. In a word, we can say that the more anyone loves himself with this inordinate self-love, the more he is his own enemy.

It is clear, then, that the destruction of self-love must precede the development of all noble human qualities and especially that it must precede all growth in the supernatural life. Only on the ruins of self-love can a noble character be built up; and, *a fortiori*, only over its ruins can the supernatural character of the new man, the man of grace, be formed. Therefore it is of the first importance that we set about freeing ourselves from inordinate self-love and self-seeking. And this we must do, insofar as it is possible for us, by means of much prayer and by a thorough disciplining of our inclinations and passions, of our pride, our self-conceit, our bad temper, our spirit of contradiction, our talkativeness, our curiosity; by obedience and by falling in entirely with community life; by showing constant charity toward our neighbor in all things. Charity—love of God and of Christ and of our neighbor—is something beautiful and great and most desirable. It protects us against self-love and drives self-love out of our souls. Indeed, only through charity can we become free from self-love; and the more charity increases in us, the more will self-love decrease.

Most of the work in the campaign against self-love, let us remember, must be done by God himself. He takes us into his own loving care and trains us in his own school, the school of suffering and humiliation: of exterior sufferings, difficulties, failures, disappointments, illness; of interior sufferings and trials, aridity, temptations of every kind. In this way he gives us a deep, salutary, experimental knowledge of our own nothingness and sinfulness and instability, and he frees us gradually of self-admiration, of inordinate self-confidence, of conceit and secret pride. It is a painful process, but it is necessary if we are to be formed into true and perfect men and wholehearted Christians.

3. "If any man come to me and hate not his father and mother and wife and children and brethren and sisters, yea and his own life too, he cannot be my disciple" (Lk 14: 26). "Every one of you that doth not

renounce all that he possesseth cannot be my disciple" (Lk 14: 33).

We have to hate ourselves in the sense Christ meant, which really means loving ourselves with a holy love that is pleasing to God. It is to be regretted that, as Father Faber says, "we are always in haste to get out of the purgative way in religion, and to enter the illuminative, just as novices wish to be out of their novitiate and long for the graver responsibilities of profession, because of its greater liberty" (F. W. Faber, *Growth in Holiness*, p. 194). And Faber further remarks that "we are especially anxious to abandon the humbling subjects of meditation." Among these subjects is self-love.

If we only look well into ourselves and see how the claims of self-love bind us, we shall gradually come to have that holy hatred of ourselves already mentioned. And so we shall be able to counteract and overcome our self-love. Our frequent Confession will help us greatly, week by week, to deepen our knowledge of ourselves. By means of it we shall learn how base and hateful and impure and insincere we are, how much in bondage and enslaved to evil self-seeking. Slowly the scales will fall from our eyes, and we shall see; we shall discover what matter of men we really are. Thus, by means of frequent Confession, we can acquire true self-knowledge and thereby attain to that hatred of ourselves which is necessary if we wish to be disciples of Christ.

And here the spiritual direction we can get from our confessor in frequent Confession will be extremely useful. It may be said that he can do us no better service than to put us on our guard against the deceptions, the deceits, and the thousands of wiles with which self-love conceals itself. Those who practice frequent Confession should seek this help from their confessor, and he ought to be able to give it to them.

Moreover, those who confess frequently will experience the power of Confession as a sacrament; through it they will have the strength of Christ, who is always our leader in the fight against sin. He and he alone is able to check and repress our self-love effectively. Through the sacrament of Penance he fills our souls with sanctifying grace and kindles charity in us until it glows and burns, especially when in conjunction with frequent Confession we daily try to prepare ourselves for a really fervent reception of Holy Communion. And where charity grows and flourishes, there must self-love disappear, just as darkness before the light.

O God, have mercy on us, absolve us from our sins,
and direct our inconstant hearts to thee. Amen.

CHAPTER THIRTEEN

Tepidity

1. A serious danger that threatens those trying to lead good and pious lives is what we call tepidity. It is, indeed, a peculiar state of the soul. The Lord has given us abundant graces and inspirations and strength; nevertheless, our spiritual growth has remained stunted. And now grace seems to produce little or no effect in us. We have become like the fig tree of the Gospel story, which our Lord saw by the wayside. "He came to it and found nothing on it but leaves only. And he saith to it: May no fruit grow on thee henceforward for ever. And immediately the fig tree withered away" (Mt 21: 19).

It is a dreadful thought that there are so many souls who begin well and fervently and successfully to lead a spiritual life and then, little by little, almost without noticing it, fall victims to tepidity. That man, that Christian, is tepid who is patient as long as he has nothing to suffer, who is meek and gentle as long as he is not contradicted, who is humble provided his reputation is not questioned in any way. That person is tepid who wishes to be a saint, without paying the price in effort and self-denial; who wants to acquire virtue, without practicing mortification; who is willing to do many things, but not to bear away the Kingdom of Heaven with violence (cf. Mt 11: 12). An inclination to omit without very much reason our practices of piety, our prayer, meditation, spiritual reading, or visits to the Blessed Sacrament, indicates tepidity. Carelessness about the so-called little things, letting the daily opportunities of doing good pass by unheeded, coming to terms with venial sin, and adopting the attitude that it is enough if we avoid mortal sin: all these are signs of tepidity.

A person cannot be reproached with being tepid on account of one single fault. Tepidity is rather a state, characterized by the fact that one, more or less deliberately, treats venial sin lightly. It is a state in which one has no zeal or fervor. Being in a state of aridity or of desolation or even feeling repugnance for the things of the spirit and of God is not tepidity; for, in spite of such feelings, the ardor of the will and the determination to do right can remain strong and steadfast. Even the fact that a person still frequently commits venial sin does not mean that he is tepid, provided he is sorry for them and fights against them. Tepidity is a state of conscious and deliberate lack of fervor, a state of lasting carelessness and half-heartedness, which pretends to justify itself by maxims such as "One should not be petty"; "God is too big and magnanimous to bother about such little things"; "Everybody else does the same"; and so on.

The danger of falling into tepidity is especially great for the man who does not keep himself steeped in the truths of the Faith and allows his whole outlook to be colored by them. God, eternity, the soul, the salvation of souls, doing God's will and pleasing God, the development of the interior life: all these mean little to such a person. His interests are in all sorts of other things: amusements, pleasure, recreation, radio, business, money-making, gaining the esteem of others. He does not want to consider his interior state. A really earnest meditation on the eternal truths is something he scarcely ever does. He prays and examines his conscience only superficially and hurriedly. He likes to busy himself with exterior occupations because he has lost his taste for the interior life. He seeks his pleasures among creatures and in his own favorite hobbies and amusements. And so the light continually grows dimmer in his soul, and his interest in, his understanding of, and his esteem for the things of God become less and less.

Then there are several other factors that, as it were, aid and abet tepidity. There is, first of all, the fact that the practice of Christian virtue is always very difficult for our fallen nature. In our spiritual striving we have to contend all the time with our own concupiscence and with many enemies and obstacles from without. We often meet with failure and defeat and disappointment. Our souls are troubled in many ways by the claims of various tasks and duties. There is the bad example of others; little by little it can lead us away from the fervor that once was ours until we too begin to take slow and weary steps along the path of virtue. Finally, there is human respect, that wretched malady that does such immeasurable damage. Indeed, to be a devout and fervent Christian requires much strength of character!

2. "Because thou art lukewarm and neither hot nor cold, I will begin to vomit thee out of my mouth" (Rev 3: 16). This is God's malediction on the tepid soul. Ought we not to do everything possible to preserve ourselves from tepidity or, if we have unfortunately fallen into that state, to arise from it, so that we may not endanger everything we value, including even our eternal salvation?

Tepidity makes us develop a perverse and false conscience, as a result of which we gradually come to look on bigger and bigger sins as mere trivialities, of no importance, scarcely venial sins. A deception, indeed, that has grave consequences! "Thou sayest: I am rich and made wealthy and have need of nothing: and knoweth not that thou art wretched and miserable and poor and blind and naked" (Rev 3: 17).

From the clouding of the judgment and of conscience there follows an increasing weakness of the will. One becomes accustomed to yielding and committing small faults: sensuality, seeking one's own comfort, bodily self-indulgence, irritability. And so, naturally, after a while one begins to be less exact also in more important things. "He that is faithful in that which is least is faithful also in that which is greater; and he that is unjust in that which is least is unjust also in that which is greater" (Lk 16: 10). Soon the will becomes so relaxed that every effort is burdensome to it. The movements and inspirations of grace are resisted, and the mind and the heart are given over to worldly things and pleasures.

This misfortune is all the more fatal and irreparable in proportion as one's downward progress is gradual and hence scarcely noticeable. One grows into the habit of continually greater and more ruinous self-deception and persuades himself that such and such things are not of any importance, that at most they are only venial sins, and so on. It is quite clear that when the spiritual life reaches this state, mortal sin is not far off.

"I have somewhat against thee, because thou hast left thy first charity. Be mindful therefore from whence thou art fallen: and do penance and do the first works. Or else I come to thee and will move the candlestick out of its place, except thou do penance" (Rev 2: 4–5). It is according to the law of nature that standing water becomes stagnant. And we know that muscles that are not exercised grow flabby and weak. It is according to the law of grace that where there is no fervor, there is no love. And, in the spiritual life, to stand still is to go backward. On the fig tree, on which he found only leaves and no fruit, Christ pronounced a terrible judgment: "May no fruit grow on thee henceforward for ever." And the result was that "immediately the fig tree withered away" (Mt 21: 19). Yes, that is tepidity: a spiritual withering away. It is not yet death, but it leads to it.

3. May God give us the grace never to sink into a state of lukewarmness or tepidity. May he give us the grace to be faithful in little things and to be watchful always and not to allow ourselves to be careless even in the smallest details. Tepidity always begins with some small carelessness that comes into our lives and then grows habitual. Every day we are guilty of carelessness in one way or another, and there is always the danger that some particular form of it will establish itself in our souls and infect them, just as the tuberculosis germ infects our bodies. To prevent this calamity we must try to have a true understanding of supernatural things and supernatural values. And the means we have at our disposal to acquire this are spiritual reading, meditation, and prayer.

A most efficacious means of preserving ourselves from the misfortune of tepidity and securing ourselves against it—or of rising out of it, if we have unfortunately fallen into that state already—is frequent Confession well made. In frequent Confession we have everything that will guard us against tepidity. For one thing, frequent Confession compels us to look into ourselves seriously to see our sins and faults, to elicit an act of contrition for them and formulate a purpose of amendment regarding them. In other words, it makes us apply ourselves with full deliberation and determination to improving our lives. Then, too, Confession is a sacrament, and, consequently, through it the power of Christ himself works in us. His greatest desire in this sacrament is to fill us with his own hatred of sin and with his own zeal to glorify his Father in all things, to be completely devoted to his service and fully resigned to his holy will. Finally, of considerable value is the direction we get from our confessor, who in every Confession will urge us anew and encourage us to continue along the way of virtue with full fervor.

One of the principal reasons for highly esteeming frequent Confession is that, when practiced as it should be, it is an infallible safeguard against tepidity. Perhaps it is this conviction that makes the Church recommend so strongly, indeed prescribe as obligation, frequent or weekly Confession for clerics and religious. Therefore, let us consider frequent Confession as something important and holy. And let us endeavor always to make our Confessions well, indeed, to try and make them better and better every time.

O God, thou makest all things work together unto
good for those who love thee. Penetrate our hearts
and fill them with unchangeable love for thee, so that
no temptation may be able to displace the desire of
thee implanted in us by thyself.

CHAPTER FOURTEEN

Sins of Omission

To him who knoweth to do good and doth it not, to him it is sin.

—JAMES 4: 17

1. We are familiar with the parable of the talents. The first servant received five talents. He traded with them and gained another five. The second servant received two talents, and he gained two more. And their lord praised each of these men, saying, "Well done, good and faithful servant." "But he that had received the one talent came and said: 'Lord, I know thou art a hard man; thou reapest where thou hast not sown and gatherest where thou hast not strewed. And being afraid, I went and hid thy talent in the earth. Behold here thou hast that which is thine.' And his lord answering, said to him: 'Wicked and slothful servant, thou knewest that I reap where I sow not and gather where I have not strewed. Thou oughtest therefore to have committed my money to the bankers: and at my coming I should have received my own with usury. Take ye away therefore the talent from him and give it to him that hath ten talents. For to everyone that hath shall be given, and he shall abound; but from him that hath not, that also which he seemeth to have shall be taken away' " (Mt 25: 24–29).

We commit sin not only be doing evil, but also by not doing the good that we can and should do, or, at any rate, by not doing it the way we could and ought to do it. This is what we mean by sins of omission: the omission of the good that in one way or another we have an obligation to do.

It is not enough that the tree exists; it must bring forth fruit and good fruit. "Every tree that bringeth not forth good fruit shall be cut down and shall be cast into the fire" (Mt 7: 19). "One day the Lord will say to those standing on his left hand: 'Depart from me. . . . For I was hungry and you gave me not to eat; I was thirsty and you gave me not to drink; I was a stranger and you took me not in. . . .' Then they shall answer him, saying: 'Lord, when did we see thee hungry or thirsty or a stranger or naked or sick or in prison and did not minister to thee?' Then he shall answer them, saying: 'Amen, I say to you, as long as you did it not to one of these least, neither did you do it to me' " (Mt 25: 41–45). These are people who do not do any evil to their neighbor. But neither do they do for him the good they could do. That is why they will be set on the left-hand side and condemned on the day of judgment.

2. We are not thinking here of the sins of omission of those who knowingly and deliberately omit the fulfillment of grave and important obligations. We are thinking rather of the sins of omission of good and fervent people, whether they be layfolk or religious or priests. The peculiar thing about such sins is that very often we pay little attention to them and do not recognize the effect they have on our spiritual life. And for that very reason they are all the more dangerous.

It must, unfortunately, be admitted that, even when we are earnestly striving to live a perfect Christian or religious life, we are daily guilty of omitting much good that we could and should do. God offers us, for instance, so many opportunities for good thoughts and pious affections. How many of these opportunities do we let pass unused, occupying ourselves instead with useless thoughts, fears, worries, and so forth! How the thought of God and of Christ ought to penetrate our whole being, influence our outlook and our aspirations, inspire our love, guide all our actions! But, alas, we omit so often to turn our thoughts to God!

Think of all our omissions with regard to opportunities for and impulses toward prayer. All those free moments we have in the course of each day: we could use them for prayer, but we omit to do so.

Think of how necessary it is for us to study deeply over and over again our holy duties as Christians or as religious, in order that we get to know them better and better: to meditate on the commandments of God and of the Church, on the obligations that we undertook in our Baptism and in our religious profession, on the rules and constitutions that declare God's will to us. No wonder that we fall into many faults and transgressions. It can scarcely be otherwise when we omit to bring home to ourselves in prayer and meditation the full implications of our vocation as Christians and as religious. He who sows not cannot expect to reap!

Think of all the inspirations of grace and all the impulses to good we neglect or to which we turn a deaf ear. We know that God is speaking to us in them and moving us, urging us on to do good. We know that "the sum of the spiritual life consists in observing the ways and the movements of the Spirit of God in our souls, and in fortifying our will in the resolution of following them" (*The Spiritual Teaching of Fr. Louis Lallement*, London, 1928, p. 113). And the same Father Lallement writes: "There are but few perfect souls, because there are but few who follow the guidance of the Holy Spirit." Another writer on the spiritual life says: "Our hope of making progress in the interior life depends entirely on the inspirations of God," that is to say, on how we attend to them and follow them.

We know all this well. And yet, although we are convinced of our great need of God's inspirations, very often we let them pass unheeded; indeed, through our neglect and indolence we gradually cause God to withdraw them from us altogether. We can do ourselves no greater injury than to let pass unheeded the inspirations and urgings of grace. They are so frequent that they accompany us, so to speak, step by step through life. They are continually streaming down upon us, like heavenly rays that shed a warm light on our hearts and show us what is good and urge us on in our spiritual striving. They enlighten our minds and move our wills: at one time to love, at another to self-denial and austerity; at one time reproaching us, at another encouraging us; at one time quietly and gently, at another strongly and intensely; sometimes just once, at other times with continual patient knocking at the door of our heart.

For how many neglected inspirations, for how many unused, rejected graces shall we have to answer! How often, alas, we are not at home when grace knocks! And when we are at home, how often do we refuse to open, so that we may be able to go our own way undisturbed, so that we may be able to act according to our whims and caprices! How often grace calls us to some sacrifice, to some act of renunciation, to some act of self-denial; and we fail to correspond with this grace. Unutilized, neglected graces! Sins of omission!

We remember Christ's parable of the sower who went out to sow his seed. One part of the seed fell by the wayside; a second part fell upon stony ground; a third part fell among briars and thorns; finally, a fourth part fell upon good ground, where it was able to grow up and bear fruit. But three-fourths of the seed remained without fruit! Is not that too the story and the mystery of the inspirations of grace in the hearts of men, which, alas, so often fail to be good ground!

Let us think especially on how thoughtlessly we let pass unused so many moments of God-given time. Every moment is a grace bestowed on us, a valuable capital entrusted to us for our use.

Finally, let us think about our behavior toward those around us, toward our neighbor. There are so many sins committed by others for which we are partly responsible. We do not wish to speak here of how often, through our conduct, our thoughtless words and remarks, our example, we are to blame for our fellow men not making use of the graces given them; of how often we are the cause of their failure to fulfill their obligations as they should. It will be sufficient to point out how badly we ourselves fail to do our duty in our relations with others. We sometimes, for instance, have the unpleasant duty of calling the attention of another—of a friend, a child, a subject, a superior, a fellow religious—to some fault. We hesitate to do so; we look on silently while others do wrong, when we could and should speak. Out of human respect we omit to correct others. We turn away and say: It is none of my business.

Again, we know what respect and what Christian charity we should show to our fellow men. We know of our duty to be reconciled with our neighbor, if we happen to quarrel with him; and we pray God to "forgive us our trespasses as we forgive them that trespass against us." We know of our duty to help and assist our fellow men and to be of service to them in every possible way. "I was hungry, I was thirsty, I was a stranger, I was naked: and you gave me to eat, you gave me to drink, and you took me in, you covered me" (cf. Mt. 25: 35–36). And there are other works of mercy it is our duty to do too: to instruct the ignorant, to counsel the doubtful, to comfort the sorrowful, to pray for all, both living and dead. How many opportunities we have! How many obligations we have! And we fail so often, without any real reason, to avail ourselves of these opportunities, to fulfill these obligations! Alas, our sins of omission!

In addition, we are often guilty of sins of omission in our relations with the society to which we belong: in our relations with our family, with our fellow parishioners, with our fellow religious, with our fellow countrymen.

What Père Lacordaire said in one of his sermons should give us serious thought: "Very few men will be able to come before God's judgment seat and say that they have not lost or at least done harm to any of those souls for whom they were responsible." And a more recent preacher warns us: "Tonight, at home in your house, when everybody has gone to sleep, go through all the rooms and imagine that all those sleepers are dead. What reproaches you would have to make to yourself: for deeds not done, for services not rendered, for words left unspoken, for kindness not shown."

3. What has been said here about the various sins of omission is not exhaustive, nor was it meant to be. Its purpose is merely to help us, especially in the practice of frequent Confession, to examine ourselves thoroughly on the omission of good in our lives and to convince us that not to do good is very often to do evil.

Moreover, one of the ways in which frequent Confession has to prove its value is in this matter of sins of omission. The person who is practicing frequent Confession must be specially watchful about neglected duties (even if, often, they are only little things), about neglected inspirations and graces, about opportunities to do good left unused, about time wasted, about failure to show charity to a neighbor. He must excite himself to a deep and sincere contrition for these omissions and to a firm resolve to strive earnestly against even the smallest of sins of omission that are in any way deliberate. If we come to Confession with this determination, we shall receive, together with the absolution pronounced by the priest, the grace to know our sins of omission better and to struggle against them more zealously. If, further, we are helped by the priest with advice and encouragement in our struggle against sins of omission, then indeed frequent Confession will become for us a most effective means of freeing ourselves, gradually, from all such faults.

May we so act that our Lord will never have to say to us what he said to Jerusalem: "How often would I . . . and thou wouldst not" (Mt 23: 37). What does he intend when he calls us, when he offers us an opportunity to do good, when he gives us some interior illumination or impulse? He wants to lead us higher, to enrich us, to make us great and blessed. But we show ourselves unwilling to respond to his love. We make ourselves guilty of sins of omission. We misuse or neglect his graces. Do we really understand what we are doing?

> *That thou wouldst keep us in thy holy service and strengthen us, we beseech thee to hear us, O Lord. From the neglect of thy inspirations, preserve us, O Lord. Make our hearts burn with the fire of thy Holy Spirit, O Lord, so that we may serve thee with chaste bodies and please thee with pure hearts.*

CHAPTER FIFTEEN

Self-Righteousness

*Now the publicans and sinners drew near unto him,
to hear him. And the Pharisees and the Scribes
murmured, saying: "This man receiveth sinners and
eateth with them." And he spoke to them this parable,
saying: "What man of you that hath a hundred
sheep, and if he shall lose one of them, doth he not
leave the ninety-nine in the desert and go after that
which was lost, until he find it? And when he hath
found it, lay it upon his shoulders, rejoicing? And
coming home, call together his friends and neighbors,
saying to them: 'Rejoice with me because I have
found my sheep that was lost?' I say to you that even
so there shall be joy in Heaven upon one sinner that
doth penance, more than upon ninety-nine just who
need not penance."*

—LUKE 15: 1–7

1. The "just" who need not penance; the just who
blame the Lord because he received sinners and ate
with them; the just who, in the proud knowledge of
their "righteousness," their sinlessness, their correctness, their blamelessness, need not penance! These are
the self-righteous.

The most repellent of all the heresies of which we
read in the history of the Church are those that tolerated no "sinners" in their fold, but, rather, boasted that

their followers consisted entirely of "saints," of the just and sinless. These "saints" looked down with contempt on the Church of Christ, which put up with so much human imperfection instead of using fire and sword to get rid of everything sinful and evil. Such were the Montanists and the Manichees and the Albigenses in former times: proud of their undefiled holiness and full of self-esteem. They vied with one another in imposing obligations and were forever hedging around the law of Christ and of the Church with new safeguards. They forbade their followers the enjoyment of meat and wine. They forbade them marriage, too, and common lowly toil. They prayed much and fasted rigorously and made a great impression on the multitude.

2. These are the self-righteous. And there are such too among Christians. Indeed, self-righteousness is precisely the sin of the pious, zealous, "correct" Christian who conscientiously and faultlessly fulfills his duty in every detail and has to reproach himself about nothing. He passes with his neighbors and superiors as an exemplary Christian—and with reason.

If only he were not so well acquainted with and so convinced of his own perfection! If only he did not think so much of himself and were not so conceited! Here danger threatens him. He knows that there is nothing to find fault with in him; he discovers nothing to reproach himself with: he has nothing to be sorry for, nothing to improve. He is one of the just "who need not penance."

The more such a man is convinced of his own "justice," the more he notices and pays attention to the sins and faults of others, of all those around him. He notices how they fail to live up to their obligations, how they transgress the Commandments of God or their rule, how they are wanting in the fulfillment of the duties of the religious life or in the fulfillment of their duties toward their fellow men, how they fall short in all sorts of ways—a thing, of course, that never happens to himself. He gets annoyed and becomes severe and hard, full of disdain and dislike toward these wrongdoers. He does not want to associate with them; he avoids them as much as he can and disregards them. Interiorly, he prides himself on his virtues and flatters himself with the thought that everyone must notice his exemplary conduct and acknowledge it and admire it. He becomes very sensitive and touchy, and he has his ways of retaliating upon those who do not recognize his merits. One of the just "who need not penance"!

The danger of self-righteousness threatens the fervent Christian who is striving to lead a good life. It threatens each of us. Quite unnoticed, self-righteousness creeps into the attitude and outlook of the Christian who is really trying to do his best and who is genuinely concerned about his progress in the spiritual life. This is especially so because always there are only relatively few who really take the Christian life seriously. All around there are baptized Christians who profess to be followers of Christ. Yet there are very many things in their daily lives that are hard to understand: so much halfheartedness; so many contradictions between their lives and the faith they profess; so much failure to produce fruit in spite of all the instruction and exhortation they receive, in spite of the good example they have before them, in spite of the lessons and admonitions they find in the books and texts of the liturgy, in spite of the meditations they make, in spite of their frequent reception of the Blessed Eucharist.

And not seldom this is true too of those who by their state in life and their holy vows have a special obligation to become perfect Christians and to lead others to the heights of the Christian life. Among these too, alas, there is so little real understanding of their vocations and so much mediocrity! What wonder if a certain feeling and conviction of moral superiority forces itself upon the person who is striving and making progress, a certain self-conceit that all too easily degenerates into self-righteousness and causes him to look down on others, to regard them with a certain disdain or with a proud sympathy.

"There shall be joy in Heaven upon one sinner that doth penance, more than upon ninety-nine just who need not penance." With these words our Lord passed judgment on self-righteousness. The self-righteous person has no need of penance or conversion. Why should he? He is already faultless and irreproachable. The knowledge that he is in every way faultless makes it impossible for him humbly to acknowledge sin, and therefore it prevents him from taking the road that leads to penance. This is the course of self-righteousness: it makes us blind to our sins and faults. Where there is no self-knowledge, there is no sense of the need for penance and no practice of penance. And where there is no sense of the need for penance, the will and the heart grow hard. God's graces and the interior inspirations of the Holy Spirit and exhortations and admonitions from outside produce no effect. Such are the just "who need not penance," who have nothing of which to repent; who, when they hear about or read about sin, never consider themselves but think only of others.

Self-righteousness is born of pride, and in turn it fosters pride and spiritual arrogance. The self-righteous man ascribes the good he sees in himself to his own efforts. He does not say with St. Paul: "By the grace of God I am what I am. And his grace in me hath not been void: but I have labored more abundantly than all they [the other Apostles]. Yet not I, but the grace of God with me" (1 Cor 15: 10). He forgets too those other words of the Apostle: "What hast thou that thou hadst not received? And if thou hast received, why dost thou glory, as if thou hadst not received it?" (1 Cor 4: 7). The self-righteous man underrates grace and its power and does an injustice to it and to him who gives it to us. Must not this conduct make him displeasing to God and cause God to withdraw gradually his grace from him? For "God resisteth the proud" (1 Pet 5: 5).

Within his heart the self-righteous man considers himself superior to others. "O God, I give thee thanks that I am not as the rest of men" (Lk 18: 11). The great masses, with whom nothing much can be done, make up "the rest of men," while he belongs to the *élite*. He knows that he is pure and perfect, while the others are far below him in the scale of virtue. "O God, I give thee thanks that I am not as the rest of men." And what is the judgment the Lord passes on him who approaches him with these dispositions? He goes down into his house without being "justified," says our Lord, "because everyone that exalteth himself shall be humbled" (Lk 18: 14). "Not as the rest of men." For these others he has in the depths of his heart only disdain and contempt. Unknown to him are the words of Christ: "Judge not: and you shall not be judged. Condemn not: and you shall not be condemned. With the same measure that you shall mete withal, it shall be measured to you again" (Lk 6: 37–38), in this life and in eternity.

Need we wonder that there is more joy in Heaven over one sinner who does penance than over ninety-nine just who need not penance? Only one thing need cause us wonder, and that is that among us Christians the vice of self-righteousness can and does exist; that there are Christians who perform their religious duties fervently, who say their prayers and receive the sacraments faithfully and who live good and decent lives, yet, in spite of all, are so blind that they do not notice how much in the depths of their hearts they consider themselves just and irreproachable and pride themselves on their fidelity and virtue.

Self-righteousness imperceptibly develops into spiritual self-assurance, as if for the devout person there were no more danger, as if he were proof against the allurements of the world and the temptations and snares of the devil, against the downward pull of his own lower nature and evil concupiscence. Such a self-assured person lives in a state of certainty about his salvation and never has a serious doubt about it. He never considers that for him, as well as for everyone else here on earth, there is always the possibility that he might prove unfaithful to his vocation, that in the face of the many obligations and sacrifices and renunciations that life imposes he might become weak, that he might fail to correspond with God's grace. He never considers that he is always liable to lapse and to fall into sins and faults unless God's grace sustains him. He acts as if the earnest warning of the Apostle did not hold for him: "With fear and trembling work out your salvation. For it is God who worketh in you, both to will and to accomplish, according to his good will" (Phil 2: 12–13). He behaves as if he did not know how insistently St. Paul reminded the Corinthians of the great graces the Lord bestowed on his people, Israel, in the crossing of the Red Sea and in the wilderness: deliverance from the power of Pharaoh, the pillar of cloud, the manna, the water out of the rock. "But," says the Apostle, "with most of them God was not well pleased: for they were overthrown in the desert. Now all these things were done in a figure of us. . . . Wherefore, he that thinketh himself to stand, let him take heed lest he fall" (1 Cor 10: 5–6, 12).

Spiritual self-assurance always causes one to go his own way in striving after Christian virtue, and the result is that, without noticing it, he is certain to go the wrong way. The self-assured person does not need anybody to warn him or advise him; he is able to look after his own affairs, and he depends on his own intelligence and good sense. Ultimately, self-assurance of this kind is a manifestation of the evil spirit of pride. But God does not allow his scheme of things to be interfered with thus with impunity: for "God resisteth the proud" (1 Pet 5: 5). And "every one that exalteth himself shall be humbled" (Lk 14: 11). Is it not terrifying to think that even an Apostle, who had lived in the closest contact with Christ, became in the end a "son of perdition" (Jn 17: 12)!

3. Against the danger of self-righteousness, which threatens in particular those who are really trying to make progress, frequent Confession, well made, is a very great help. The better we practice it, the more surely will it be for us a way to fuller and deeper self-knowledge and to the recognition of our imperfection and sinfulness. It will uncover for us the wounds of our soul and make us recognize that we still "offend in many things" (James 3: 2) and that we never have grounds for considering ourselves just and perfect or for looking down on others and on their religious practice. If, moreover, we have a sympathetic confessor who will help us toward a deeper understanding and a more fruitful practice of Confession, then indeed, as a result of frequent Confession, we can scarcely fail to develop more and more a true spirit of penance and an ardent desire for more perfect purity of soul and more perfect charity.

Lord, "what is man that thou art mindful of him?"
(Ps 8: 4). What good has man done that thou
shouldst give him thy grace? In truth I can only
think and say: Lord, I am nothing; I can do
nothing; of myself I have no good in me. Rather, I
am weak in all things and tend to nothingness.
Unless I am helped and instructed by thee, I become
utterly indifferent and wicked.

Thanks be to thee, from whom all comes whenever I
am successful. I am vanity itself and as nothing
before thee. In what, then, can I take pride? Truly,
vainglory is the greatest folly. For as long as a man is
pleasing to himself he is displeasing to thee. But there
is true glory and a holy joy in glorying in thee and
not in oneself, in rejoicing in thy name and not in
one's own strength. Praised be thy name, not mine.
May thy work be glorified, not mine. Thou art my
glory and the joy of my heart. In thee will I glory and
rejoice the whole day long. In myself I will not glory,
except in my infirmities.

—*Imitation of Christ*, BK. 3, CH. 40

CHAPTER SIXTEEN

Contrition

I

And Peter remembered the word of Jesus which He had said: "Before the cock crow, thou will deny me thrice," and going forth, he wept bitterly.

— MATTHEW 26: 75

"Going forth, he wept bitterly." Peter, the rock, who only just before was on fire with holy zeal for his lord and master, who in the Garden of Gethsemane boldly stood up for Christ, who with sincere love and concern followed him to the house of the High Priest when he was arrested—this same Peter denied Jesus. "I know not this man" (Mt 26: 72). "And the Lord turning looked on Peter. And Peter remembered the word of the Lord" (Lk 22: 61). The look of Jesus opened his eyes. Now he sees what he has done. What can he do about it?

"Going forth, he wept bitterly." Now he sees how he has behaved toward his Lord, whom he once solemnly acknowledged as "Christ, the Son of the Living God" (Mt 16: 16) and who had chosen him in preference to the other Apostles to be the rock on which he would build his Church. Now he does not want to admit that he knows him, him whom formerly he followed everywhere joyfully and faithfully, whose miracles he had seen with his own eyes, on whom he had gazed on Mount Tabor, with whom just previously he had partaken of the Last Supper. "I know not this man."

"Going forth, he wept bitterly." Now he sees what he had done. He understands what sin means, and he cannot bear its weight. It burns his soul like a painful wound. It drives him forth. He flies from the occasion of sin. He must atone for his lapse; he must do penance. How his sin grieves him! How it burns his soul! How all the circumstances that led him to sin disgust him now!

What is contrition? Are Peter's tears, perhaps, his contrition? No; contrition is something interior. Does Peter's contrition consist in the fact that he now feels deep disgrace for having so forgotten himself, that he feels ashamed of himself and ashamed before others? No; it is not this either. Perhaps his contrition is the fear that Christ will now deprive him of the promised primacy in his Church, that he will confer it on a more faithful Apostle? No; contrition is sorrow of soul for sin that has been committed, together with a firm purpose not to commit it any more.

Sin is a rebellion against the all-holy God. When we sin our will sets itself against God, transgresses his command. Contrition fills the will with a deep sorrow for revolting thus against God and treating him so badly. It means that we regret that we have trampled God's command underfoot, that we have sinned, that we have offended God. It means that we are determined to break with that way of acting and with the dispositions that led to it, even if that involves a big sacrifice.

Genuine contrition does not consist merely in saying "I should like not to have done it." Nor is it a sensation, an emotional feeling of sorrow, something felt in the senses. No, contrition need not necessarily be felt in the senses at all. It is in the will. It is a purely spiritual thing, a determination of the will—which may or may not be accompanied by feelings of sorrow. It is a true, genuine change of disposition, such as took place in the case of St. Peter. The will, which before adhered to something evil, now casts this from it, hates it, abhors it, and feels repugnance toward it. It wishes that evil undone and would undo it if it could. Thus, contrition necessarily includes the determination not to do any more the evil that has been done and to take the means to avoid it in the future (purpose of amendment).

Contrition is of the very essence of penance and is the most important of the various acts that are necessary for the reception of the sacrament of Penance. Without it there is no forgiveness of sin, no fruitful or worthy confession. If all those who go to Confession frequently would only concentrate more on deepening their contrition, they would derive much more profit from their confessions.

"And the Lord turning looked on Peter." This grace-laden look of Christ must have touched the heart of poor Peter. Immediately "going forth, he wept." The contrition that is profitable for our souls is excited under the influence and stimulation of grace; it is the fruit, not of any natural activity or purely natural efforts of ours, but of grace and of prayer. It is of supernatural origin, and consequently it must be sought for in prayer.

Genuine contrition is also supernatural in its motive. A person who is sorry for sin and unfaithfulness only because these things are ugly in themselves, or because they are so unbecoming in a Christian or in a religious, or because they involve him in some humiliation or put him in an embarrassing situation before others—such a person has only a natural sorrow for sin and not the true contrition that is necessary for forgiveness.

"And going forth." St. Peter's contrition is efficacious: it leads to action. St. Peter goes away from the surroundings and company that were an occasion of sin to him and returns to them no more. He leaves the place where he proved disloyal to his Lord and makes satisfaction for his sin by his ardent zeal for Christ and for Christ's interests and by his whole life and his death for Christ.

It is sometimes objected against frequent Confession that, precisely on account of its frequency, it is almost inevitable that it will be made mechanically and out of routine and, consequently, that it will not produce much result. It is true that there is this danger in the practice of frequent Confession. But there is exactly the same danger in frequent and daily Holy Communion, in the daily celebration of Holy Mass, in the daily recitation of the Breviary and of other fixed prayers. Is the danger of routine, then, to be eliminated by going to Holy Communion less frequently, by celebrating Mass and praying one's Breviary less often? Certainly not.

In the case of frequent Confession the danger of routine will be warded off if we put the emphasis not on confession—on the actual accusation of sins—but rather fully and entirely on deepening and enlivening our contrition and on perfecting our purpose of amendment. Our accusation of sins will probably not vary very much, as a rule; the further we advance the more likely we are to have pretty much the same to confess every time. Consequently, it is all the more important that we try to develop and improve our contrition.

With this in view, in each Confession our contrition should cover not merely the sins we have actually confessed but, as well, each and every sin and unfaithfulness of our whole past life. In this way we shall be able without difficulty to develop our practice of frequent Confession so that it will be safeguarded against the danger of becoming mechanical and will be a really useful and fruitful practice for the life of our souls.

We beseech thee, O Lord, to hear our humble supplication and to show unto us thy unbounded mercy. Forgive us all our sins and remit the punishment that we deserve on account of them. Amen.

II

"Then, when I was condemned by the judge to the infamous death of the cross and the royal standard laid on my shoulders, I was ignominiously led forth and publicly mocked. Wherever I walked, my footprints could be recognized there by my blood. The Jews shouted at me fiercely along the way, so that the cry rose on the ear: Death, death to the evil-doer. With criminals and thieves I was led along to the place of execution. Then I was stripped and stretched out on the cross, which lay on the ground. My hands and my feet were bound to the beams of the cross with ropes and then cruelly fastened with nails. The cross was lifted up and on it I hung, shamefully, between Heaven and earth.

"Now behold me on the high scaffold of the cross. My right hand was nailed through, and my left hand also was pierced. My right arm was stretched out, and my left arm was painfully extended. My right foot was dug through, and my left foot also was cruelly transfixed. I hung on the cross helpless, my divine limbs overcome with weariness. All my tender limbs were pressed immovably to the hard rack of the cross. My warm blood was forced out wildly in many places, so that my dying body was covered with it and made all bloody and a pitiable sight. And behold, a lamentable thing! My young body, in the prime of life, began to wither away and to be parched and famished. . . . My whole body was wounded through and through and full of pain. . . . My clear eyes became dim. . . . My ears were filled with mockery and insults. . . . Everything of earth was wanting to me, even a little peace. My divine head was bowed with pain and calamity. My pure countenance was defiled with spittle, and my clear complexion was become pale. Behold, my beautiful form had disappeared; it was as if I were a leper and had never been the all-beautiful Word of God. Indeed, the light of Heaven was extinguished out of sympathy for me, from the sixth hour onward.

"In the greatest anguish and mortal distress I hung there wretchedly before my executioners; and they stood before me and called out to me in cruel mockery. They wagged their heads at me insultingly, and in their hearts they set me at naught, just as if I were a miserable worm. But all the while I stood firm and prayed lovingly to my heavenly Father for them. Behold how I, the innocent lamb, was numbered with the guilty! I was mocked by one of them. But the other called on me for help. And I answered him immediately and forgave him all his misdeeds; I opened to him the gates of Paradise. Yes, in my unfathomable mercy I prayed lovingly to my Father for those who had crucified me, for those who divided my garments amongst themselves, and for those who blasphemed me, the King of Kings, as I suffered most cruelly and was most disgracefully mocked.

"But hear this lamentable thing! I looked about me, forsaken as I was by all mankind, and even the friends who had followed me as disciples now stood afar off. . . . I hung there . . . stripped of my garments. I had become powerless and without might. They showed me no mercy. . . . I was overwhelmed with anguish of heart and bitter distress wherever I turned. My sorrowful Mother stood beneath my cross and the torments I was suffering rent her maternal heart with pain.

"And as I hung there so completely helpless and forsaken, with the blood dripping down from my wounds, with the tears falling from my eyes, with arms stretched out and the veins in all my members distorted in the agony of death: I raised my voice pitifully and in my misery called upon my Father and said: 'My God, my God, why hast thou forsaken me!' Behold, when my blood had all ebbed away and my strength had failed in my death agony, I was stricken with severe thirst; but I thirsted still more for the salvation of all men. Then, to assuage this terrible thirst, gall and vinegar were offered to my parched lips. And at last when the redemption of mankind was fully accomplished, I cried out: *'Consummatum est!* It is consummated!' And so, having shown perfect obedience to my Father, even unto death, I commended my spirit into his hands, saying 'Into thy hands I commend my spirit.' And then my noble soul departed from my divine body.

"Afterward my right side was pierced with a sharp spear. And there came forth a stream of my precious blood and together with it a fountain of living water that would restore to life all that were dead or withered and would slake the thirsty hearts of men."

—Denifle, *Das geistliche Leben*, II, part 2, ch. 4

Learn from the sight of your crucified Savior what sin is. All this was necessary to make atonement for sin. You could not do it; the whole world could not do it. Heaven and earth could not do it; only God in human form could do it. Such is sin's terrible malice against God. "Acknowledge that you brought Christ to the cross, that you caused your Savior these unspeakable pains and this cruel death. Consider how by every [mortal] sin you crucify again the Son of God" (Heb 6: 6). Is this what he has deserved from you? Recognize the error of your ways and your ungratefulness. With Mary

Magdalene kneel as a penitent at the feet of the Crucified and bewail your misdeeds. Weep for all the sins of
your whole life.

Then present yourself to your Savior, and he will address to you through the mouth of his representative
those words of comfort: "I absolve thee from thy sins."

O Lord God, graciously pour forth into our hearts
the grace of the Holy Spirit. May it enable us with
sighs and tears to wash away the stains of our sins
and to obtain the forgiveness for which we long.
Amen.

III

1. The punishment for venial sin is not eternal, as is
the case for mortal sin, but temporal; and satisfaction
can be made for venial sin by our acceptance of the
various sufferings and trials of this present life. But
whatever debt of temporal punishment still remains at
the end of life goes with the soul through the gates of
death and has to be paid fully in the next life: in Purgatory.

God is infinitely holy and just! He loves greatly the
soul that has departed this earthly life in the state of
grace. He sees it as redeemed with the blood of Christ.
He sees it as infinitely loved by his Divine Son, as mysti-
cally espoused to him, who gave his life for it and who
united it most closely to himself in holy Baptism. He
sees it as loved by the Holy Spirit, who gave himself to it,
who took up his abode in it, and who pleaded for it
"with unspeakable groanings" (Rom 8: 26). He has already prepared a place in Heaven for this soul and
looks forward with joy to the moment when he will be
able to receive it and lead it in and set on its head the
crown of glory. Then would he invite all the inhabitants

of Heaven to rejoice with him on account of this happy soul that has now become a sharer in eternal bliss.

But as much as God loves such a soul, as much as he longs to have it with himself, he must keep it away until it has paid "the last farthing" (Mt 5: 26), that is, until it has undergone the full punishment due for its sins. How seriously God takes sin, even venial sin!

2. And what terrible punishment and atonement! The punishment of fire! A fire has the power to lay hold of the soul, to enter into it and penetrate it and to produce in its every part the sharpest torments. A fire that distinguishes between him who sinned once and him who sinned often; between those who sinned through frailty and thoughtlessness and those who sinned through deliberate carelessness and with full knowledge.

And then there is "the pain of loss." It is the great spiritual martyrdom of the souls suffering in this place of purification. They are now free from the bonds of sense and of the body; they are removed from earth's illusions and pretense, from its enticements and seductions, from its distractions and diversions. Now they feel themselves irresistibly drawn toward God. The soul knows nothing else and feels the need of nothing else except God. It now sees clearly that God alone is its true good, its sole source of happiness. With all the ardor of which it is capable it wants to cast itself into the heart of God, to embrace him, to find peace in him. But it is shut out from him. The doors are barred, and it must go away. It knocks, it weeps, it prays—but in vain. What a terrible frustration! "Thou shall not go out from thence till thou repay the last farthing" (Mt 5: 26). That is what venial sin is in the sight of the all-holy and all-just God.

How the soul yearns for Christ, its Savior! Is not he its only thought, its only desire? If only it could be with him and share his happiness! "Come to me, all you that labor and are burdened, and I will refresh you" (Mt 11: 28). But in this life it did not correspond fully with grace; it was guilty of so much carelessness and half-heartedness; it refused to sacrifice everything for the love of its Savior. Now, in the light of eternity, it recognizes its ingratitude and unfaithfulness toward Christ. It recognizes that its protestations of love for him and for him alone were often insincere and were given the lie by its actions. It laments bitterly now its superficiality, indecision, laziness, cowardice, self-seeking, its coldness and ungratefulness toward Christ. How the thought of the cross, the tabernacle, the altar pains it now! What powerful means it had in them, while still on earth, to save itself from the pains of Purgatory! But it did not use them properly. It could have done so, if it had really been in earnest. Now, alas, it is too late!

This is the punishment of venial sin. If only the tears of contrition could wash away its stains, as they can while we are here on earth! But the time of merit has now passed. The pains and torments of Purgatory cannot merit any remission. "The night cometh when no man can work" (Jn 9: 4). Now there is only one thing: suffering and nothing but suffering, until, by suffering alone, "the last farthing" is paid. The soul prays—but that does not avail it any longer. It loves its Lord our God—but that brings no alleviation or shortening of its suffering. It bears its suffering patiently—but all its resignation and patience can no longer obtain for it any consolation or mercy. Helpless, it is given over to suffering until "the last farthing" is paid.

How long will that be? "Till thou repay the last farthing." What frightful words! What a frightful, mysterious, terrifying duration! That is the result of the unfaithfulness and sin that here on earth are treated so lightly! How our eyes will be opened in Purgatory! O that we could see things now in this life in the same clear way!

3. The practice of frequent Confession aims at keeping us free from the guilt of venial sin and therefore from the punishment that follows it: in other words, it aims at preserving us from the fire of Purgatory. Yes, frequent Confession will help to keep us out of Purgatory. It is true that during our life on earth we shall never be entirely free from sins of frailty. These sins, however, are not as a rule fully deliberate. They are not really indicative of our dispositions toward God and do not imply that love for him is wanting in us. Consequently, their guilt and the punishment due to them can easily be remitted while we are still here on earth by the many acts of love and of other virtues that we perform every day, by the reception of the Holy Eucharist, by the indulgences the Church grants us.

As regards deliberate sin, frequent Confession, if properly made, forces us to strive with all our strength to eradicate sin and to lead a life of perfect love of God. If we are really advanced to the state where we love God above all things, where our hearts are no longer so set on anything created that we are not ready to sacrifice it for the sake of God; if, with God's grace, we have arrived at a state when we accept everything from God, just as he gives it or takes it—wealth or poverty, honor or contempt, health or sickness; if, out of love for God, we are ready to lay down our life, were God to ask it: then it should be in no way impossible for us to come to the blessed possession of God after death without having to pass through the fires of Purgatory. By means of frequent Confession, well made, together with frequent Holy Communion and an earnest and constant striving to grow in the holy love of

God, we may indeed expect to attain this high and mature state in the spiritual life.

Our chances of going straight to Heaven after death are increased if during life we esteem and reverently make use of the indulgences the Church grants in order to help us cancel out the temporal punishment due to our sins—for Purgatory is part of that temporal punishment. And if, in addition, God gives us the opportunity to receive the sacrament of Anointing of the Sick, which takes away the remains of sin—"*peccati reliquias abstergit,*" as the Council of Trent says—and opens Heaven's door, as it were, for us: then, indeed, we may well hope to escape Purgatory altogether. Here is how one spiritual writer puts it:

"As the life of grace is essentially ordained to that of glory, the normal, although in fact quite rare, summit of its development should be a very perfect disposition to receive the light of glory immediately after death without passing through Purgatory; for it is only through our own fault that we will be detained in that place of expiation, where the soul can no longer merit.

"Now, this very perfect disposition to immediate glorification can be nothing other than an intense charity coupled with the ardent desire of the Beatific Vision, such as we find them particularly in the transforming union, after the painful passive purifications which have delivered the soul from its blemishes. Since nothing unclean can enter Heaven, in principle a soul must undergo these passive purifications at least in a measure before death while meriting and progressing, or after death without meriting or progressing" (R. Garrigou-Lagrange, O.P., *Christian Perfection and Contemplation*, London, 1937, p. 128).

Frequent Confession can help us greatly to attain this deeply rooted love, and thus, when used together

with the other means—the sacraments and indulgences—it can enable us, not merely to escape Purgatory, but to live a life that for all eternity will honor and
glorify God ever so much more than if we had not
reached these heights of love. What a great good frequent Confession can be for us if we understand it and
try to make our Confessions well!

> *Give us, O Lord, the grace to love that which thou*
> *commandest and to desire that which thou dost*
> *promise, so that amid all the vicissitudes of this life*
> *our hearts may be firmly fixed where true happiness is*
> *to be found.*

CHAPTER SEVENTEEN

Compunction of Heart

A humble and contrite heart thou wilt not despise, O God.

1. One of the precious fruits of frequent Confession is, naturally, the growth of a spirit of compunction, that is, a lasting sorrow of soul for the sins one has committed. The masters of the spiritual life emphasize the great importance of compunction of heart for Christian thinking and living. They recognize the great value of this attitude of soul, which makes us habitually feel sentiments of contrition for past sin, even long after we have received pardon from God.

It is very moving to see how the great Apostle, St. Paul, thanks his Lord, Jesus Christ, for numbering him among his followers and selecting him for the ministry, him "who before was a blasphemer and a persecutor and contumelious. But I obtained the mercy of God, because I did it ignorantly in unbelief. . . . A faithful saying and worthy of all acceptation: that Christ Jesus came into the world to save sinners, of whom I am the chief" (1 Tim 1: 13, 15). How the sorrowful memory of those things in which he had sinned many years before remained alive in Paul! "I am the least of the apostles, who am not worthy to be called an apostle, because I persecuted the Church of God" (1 Cor 15: 9). The more vivid his consciousness of having formerly persecuted the Lord (cf. Acts 9: 4–5), the more he feels himself compelled to spend himself and all his strength for the Lord and for his interests and to give everything, unto the last, even unto his very blood and life, for him.

There is a tradition that St. Peter, the chief of the Apostles, bewailed his whole life long the sin he committed when he denied his Master in the house of the High Priest. Sorrow for his sin became for him a spur urging him to labor and sacrifice for Christ and his Church, to unshakable fidelity in his office of Apostle and Head of the Church, and, eventually, to the shedding of his blood in testimony to his Lord.

In the daily celebration of the Eucharistic sacrifice the Church never tires of trying to develop this spirit of compunction in both priest and congregation and to deepen it in them. Recall, for instance, from the *Missale Romanum*, the prayer as the priest ascends the altar ("Take away from us our iniquities, we beseech thee, O Lord . . ."), the offering of the bread at the Offertory ("Accept . . . this immaculate host which I, Thy unworthy servant, offer Thee . . ."), after the Consecration the *Nobis quoque peccatoribus* ("Also to us sinners . . ."). The Church well knows that God does not despise a contrite heart, and therefore she puts on our lips the prayer: "In the spirit of humility and with a contrite heart may we be received by thee, O Lord." And again, every day in the Divine Office, as the Church has prescribed it in the Breviary, we find this same concern about the spirit of compunction: in the Psalms, in the lessons, in the prayers. The Church recognizes that continual and lasting sorrow of the soul for the sins we have committed is something very important.

The saints have all been taught by the Church and have learned this lesson from her. That is why a soul as pure as St. Gertrude can pray: "My Lord, amongst the remarkable wonders thou dost work, I consider especially great the fact that this earth supports me, miserable sinner that I am." In this St. Gertrude shows herself to be a true disciple of St. Benedict, the father of Western monasticism. St. Benedict directs his sons "daily in their prayers, with tears and sighs, to confess their sins to God and to amend those sins for the future" (*The Rule of St. Benedict*, ed. and trans. by Abbot Justin McCann, London, 1952, ch. 4). "Let us be sure," he says, "that we shall not be heard for our much speaking, but for purity of heart and tears of compunction" (ch. 20). The attitude a monk should have is described by him in the words: "A monk should . . . always have his head bowed and his eyes downcast, pondering always the guilt of his sins, and considering that he is about to be brought before the dread judgment seat of God" (ch. 7: the twelfth degree of humility). The great saint and doctor of the Church, Augustine, writes similarly that "God sees our tears. Our sighs do not go unheard by him who created everything by his word and who has no need of our human words." Therefore, prayer consists not in multiplying words but rather "in sighs and tears" (Epistle 180, 10).

A woman once wrote to Pope St. Gregory the Great saying that she would give him no peace until he assured her, on God's behalf, that her sins were forgiven. St. Gregory replied to her that he did not consider himself worthy to receive revelations from God and that, moreover, it was more salutary for her soul that up to the last moment of her life she should be without absolute certainty of forgiveness. He recommended her to live always in the spirit of compunction until her last hour was come and never to let a day go by without bewailing her sins with tears (Epistle 7: 25). Such are the sentiments of holy souls.

St. Teresa of Avila had always before her eyes in her cell the words of the psalmist: "Enter not into judgment with thy servant, O Lord" (Ps 143: 2). Thus did this great teacher of prayer and of the interior life sum up all her prayers: not in a protestation of love but in a cry of compunction. And it is not a question of single, passing acts of sorrow or of feelings of sorrow lasting such a short time; it is a lasting interior disposition, which reveals itself exteriorly too. The same St. Teresa, speaking of souls favored by God with special graces, tells us that "the more they receive from our God, the greater grows their sorrow for sin." "I believe myself," she adds, "that this will never leave us until we reach that place, where nothing can cause us affliction" (*Interior Castle, Sixth Mansion*, ch. 7). We ought, indeed, to pay much heed to those words of the saint: . . . "The more they receive from our God, the greater grows their sorrow for sin." And we can add too that the more one fosters the spirit of contrition and of compunction, the more graces will one receive from God.

2. What then is this compunction, this lasting sorrow of soul for the sins we have committed? St. Teresa herself tells us in the same place: "The soul does not now think of the pain it is bound to suffer on account of its sins, but only of how ungrateful it has been to him to whom it owes so much, and who so greatly merits our service. . . . It is aghast at having been so bold; it weeps for its lack of reverence; its foolish mistakes in the past seem to it to have been so gross that it cannot stop grieving, when it remembers that it forsook so great a Majesty for things so base."

The more a soul draws near to God, the more it perceives its defects and faults, and the clearer it understands the malice of its former sins: its mortal sins, its venial sins, its sins of frailty, and its imperfections. Every day it regrets more that it sinned thus and develops such an aversion to everything that displeases God that it becomes more and more incapable of being unfaithful or of being guilty of faults that are in any way deliberate. It becomes so sensitive and delicate with regard to God that henceforth it can live only according to his holy will.

Compunction, lasting sorrow of soul for past sins, consists in the continual feeling and realization that we are sinners, without, however, recalling any of our sins in particular. It consists in our begging for forgiveness unceasingly, though with full confidence. "Wash me yet more from my iniquity, and cleanse me from my sin" (Ps 50: 2). It consists in concern about past sins that have been forgiven, in the sense that one is always conscious of how easily old bad habits and failings reassert themselves and put us in danger of falling again. It consists especially in a continually increasing hatred of sin, of even the smallest sin or unfaithfulness, and in a growing delicacy of conscience. We draw near to God and consequently with his divine light we see more clearly what is imperfect and unworthy and displeasing to God both in our interior life and in our external behavior. We come to recognize how frequently our motives are imperfect, and we feel ourselves compelled more and more to act from the motive of love. And all the time we are increasing in gratitude and love to God, who forgives us our sins, and to Christ our Savior, who delivered us from sin.

Compunction grows from the consciousness that by our sins we have offended the infinitely good God, that we have treated him unjustly, that we have put him second to our own pleasure, that we have harmed his interests and detracted from his glory. Therefore compunction is really nothing else but an expression of our perfect sorrow and one of the most genuine forms of the love of God. It is, too, a spur that urges us on continually to make up for the past by all the greater faithfulness now. Out of grateful love for God, who mercifully forgives him the former unfaithfulness, the person who has the spirit of compunction strives earnestly against all deliberate levity of spirit and habitual frivolity.

Compunction will not tolerate any indiscipline where the things of God are concerned, nor will it allow tepidity to creep in. It inclines us to receive the sacraments with ever greater humility and reverence—and therefore with greater fruit. It gives us strength for all the interior and exterior trials to which God subjects us and gives us the courage and the steadfastness to face willingly the sacrifices and renunciations and labors and burdens of life. It is, indeed, a sorrow not unto death but, rather, unto life: lasting, tranquil, supernatural; a spring from which love issues. It is a sorrow that is peaceful and gentle and that can be with us without making us weak and feeble. It is a humble sorrow, but not one that causes us to be downcast or dejected on account of our faults. It nourishes itself on a holy reverence for God's inscrutable judgments; it brings consolation into our prayer; it is full of trust in God's mercy and full of a holy gratitude.

This loving sorrow tempers and softens our character; it makes us sympathetic and compassionate and tolerant toward others; it inclines us to put the best construction on the faults and failings of others and to judge them kindly. It bestows on us the gift of genuine interior piety and prevents us from going through our daily work and prayer in a merely routine and mechanical way. It secures us against the danger of treating venial sin lightly and consequently becomes for us a very powerful means toward living a holy life. In particular, it gives our spiritual campaigning constancy and steadfastness and preserves us from that harmful vacillation and irresolution which so frequently endanger our interior progress. It is the great means for making our spiritual life solid and steady.

3. Compunction of heart is, indeed, something great and valuable. It is to be regretted that today, in certain circles, the word "compunction" and the thing signified by this word meet with little approval—if they are not rejected entirely. People today desire a "positive" spirituality. And rightly so. It is certainly right to call attention to and to make use of everything that is elevating, that fosters freedom and happiness, that is beautiful and triumphant in our Catholic faith. And this is especially true with regard to the religious training of young people.

His Holiness, Pope Pius XII, in a letter to the German bishops gathered at Fulda in 1940, recognized expressly the legitimacy of this endeavor. It would be, however, he added, "a fatal mistake to think that the results of such an endeavor could be enhanced by putting less stress on the necessity to watch and pray (Mk 14: 38), which the Divine Master so earnestly inculcated."

It is good and it is important to emphasize the positive side of spirituality: charity, prayer, realization of our divine sonship by adoption, our membership in Christ's Mystical Body. It would, however, be fatal to forget that all this is possible only in a soul that has been purified from sin and sinful habits and from all inordinate attachments; in a soul that continually strives, by a life of vigilance and self-discipline, to dam up the sources of sin and imperfection.

It is a depressing fact that the spiritual life of many pious people, indeed of many of those consecrated to

God, is so wavering and unsteady; that so many honestly strive to attain the heights of the spiritual life, and that nevertheless so few reach them; that so many are called to union with God, and that so few live up to that vocation; that so many begin to build with genuine zeal, and yet death finds them with the building incomplete, if not, perhaps, collapsed.

We may ask what is the reason for these and similar phenomena. One well-versed in matters of the interior life pondered this question for many years and decided ultimately that the source of this interior inconstancy, by which spiritual progress is so often held up and endangered, is the lack of the spirit of compunction. This much, at least, is certain: the surest way to make our spiritual life secure and constant, tranquil and steadfast, is to cultivate a spirit of compunction: the lasting supernatural sorrow for the sins we have committed. "To them that love God all things work together unto good" (Rom 8: 28), even the sins that they bewail and ever continue to bewail anew. *O felix culpa*—O happy fault!

This spirit of compunction must be the special fruit that the practice of frequent Confession produces in us. To achieve this, two things are important and should be noted.

First of all, we who have been given the grace to practice frequent Confession must resolutely and as a matter of principle set our face against the attitude that would regard venial sin as a harmless trifle: as if, fundamentally, it were something that did not make any difference with regard to the glory and interests of God and of Christ and to our supernatural life and progress; as if it were, as a Catholic theologian attempted to show recently, not forbidden but rather "tolerated" by God. It is clear that in such views there is little place either for the practice of frequent Confession or for the spirit of compunction.

Secondly, in our Confession we must put the emphasis on contrition. And in order to excite ourselves to a contrition that will be as perfect as possible, let us include in it, at least in a general way, all the sins of our whole past life. The more we try to develop our contrition in this way in our Confession, the more securely will an enduring sorrow for our past sins become established in our lives. If, moreover, as we review the day each evening in our examination, we emphasize contrition and try to develop it in the same way, then we may certainly expect that God will pour forth the spirit of compunction into our hears.

It is very important too that we should accustom ourselves to consider our crucified Savior, who, as our representative, made satisfaction to God's offended justice. It should be the same with us as with St. Angela of Foligno. To her the Lord said: "Not just as a jest have I loved thee!" "These words," wrote St. Angela, "pierced my soul like a deadly pain. With a dreadfully serious love has Christ loved me! And how my own love for him seemed to me like a joke in bad taste, like a lie. I have never loved thee except in jest and in pretense, and I have never been willing to carry the cross with thee." St. Angela is indeed now filled with the spirit of compunction; henceforth she wants only to love and, out of love, to suffer. That was the lesson she learned in the school of the Crucified, and we can learn there too how to acquire the spirit of compunction and how to deepen and make fruitful our practice of frequent Confession.

Wash me yet more from my iniquity, and cleanse me
from my sin. Thou shall sprinkle me with hyssop,
and I shall be cleansed. Turn away thy face from my

*sins and blot out my iniquities. Create a clean heart
in me and renew a right spirit within my bowels.
Cast me not away from thy face and take not thy holy
Spirit from me. A sacrifice to God is an afflicted
spirit; a contrite and humbled heart, O God, thou
wilt not despise.*

—PSALM 51: 2–17

CHAPTER EIGHTEEN

Sacramental Satisfaction

I chastise my body and bring it into subjection: lest perhaps, when I have preached to others, I myself should become a castaway.

— 1 CORINTHIANS 9: 27

1. It is the teaching of the Church that God forgives the sinner the guilt of mortal sin and, with the guilt, the eternal punishment due to it (the punishment of Hell) in such a way that temporal punishment still remains to be undergone. By temporal punishment is meant punishment through works of penance undertaken in this life or, where these are not sufficient, through suffering endured hereafter in Purgatory. Thus, for instance, in the case of our first parents, God forgave their sin and the eternal punishment of Hell due to it; but at the same time he decreed a temporal punishment for them. "I will multiply thy sorrows, and thy conceptions," God said to Eve; "in sorrow shalt thou bring forth children." And to Adam he said: "Cursed is the earth in thy work. With labor and toil shalt thou eat thereof all the days of thy life. Thorns and thistles shall it bring forth to thee. In the sweat of thy face shalt thou eat bread till thou return to the earth, out of which thou wast taken: for dust thou art, and into dust thou shalt return" (Gen 3: 16–19). The Bible tells us a similar story about Moses and Aaron. The people of Israel

were without water in the wilderness and were in danger of dying from thirst. Then Moses and Aaron prayed to God, and Moses received from God the order: "Take the rod, assemble the people together, thou and Aaron thy brother: and speak to the rock before them and it shall yield waters. And when thou hast brought forth water out of the rock, all the multitude and their cattle shall drink." Then Moses took the rod, and he and Aaron gathered together the multitude before the rock, and Moses spoke to them saying: "Hear ye, rebellious and incredulous. Can we bring you forth water out of this rock?" And Moses struck the rock twice with the rod, and water gushed forth in great abundance. But the Lord said to Moses and Aaron: "Because you have not believed me, to sanctify me before the children of Israel, you shall not bring these people into the land, which I will give them" (Nb 20: 2–12). The guilt of their sin was forgiven by God to Moses and Aaron; but they were punished for doubting God's power by not being allowed to enter the Land of Promise.

St. Paul the Apostle pointed out sternly to the Corinthians that there were "many infirm and weak" among them and that "many slept." They were judged by the Lord for this. "But whilst we are judged, we are chastised by the Lord, that we be not condemned with this world" (1 Cor 11: 30–32). Even when the sin is forgiven there still remains due to it a debt of punishment that can be paid by enduring the various sufferings of this world and the pains of death.

All this holds good for mortal sin. It holds good also, in due proportion, for venial sin. In Confession, God, through the absolution pronounced by his representative, the priest, forgives us the guilt of the venial sins we have confessed and for which we are sorry; and with the guilt, he forgives too at least a part of the temporal punishment due to them. But it must often happen that God does not forgive all the temporal punishment and this for good reasons.

When we commit venial sin we do not, it is true, turn away entirely from God, as in the case of mortal sin. We remain, as it were, still on the road that leads to him, and our steps are still directed toward him. But we attach ourselves excessively to some creature, to something that seems to be to our own advantage, to some inordinate pleasure or gratification. This inordinate surrender to something created, to ourselves, to excessive gratification of one kind or another, deserves to be punished and calls for expiation. And it is fittingly expiated when those very things to which we were excessively attached and which we sought and made use of in an inordinate way are withdrawn from us; when we are afflicted with all sorts of temporal evils and sufferings and illnesses and losses and trials and thus chastised by God here in order "that we be not condemned with this world" (1 Cor 11: 32); when we become disgusted with the very things to which we surrendered ourselves inordinately or lose them entirely.

Such trials and sufferings are good for us. They keep us conscious of our faults and make us watchful over ourselves. By thus humbly undergoing punishment for our sins, we become more detached and purer and more determined to lead good lives. In particular, works of penance and atonement make us more like our suffering, atoning Lord and Savior Christ, our Head, and unite us to him, from whom our acts of penance derive all their value and effectiveness.

2. It is the teaching of the Church that the priest, in virtue of the office of judge, which he exercises in the sacrament of Penance, has the right to impose certain works of penance—a "sacramental penance" as we

say—that will help to cancel the debt of temporal punishment due to sin. Indeed, it is his duty to do so, out of the holy care he must have for those souls he absolves in this tribunal. Besides, it will naturally be his greatest desire that his penitent should be freed from punishment as well as from guilt. It follows that the penitent has an obligation to accept the penance imposed by the confessor and to perform it.

Wherever there is genuine contrition and an interior turning away from sin, there also will be found readiness to do penance and make satisfaction, readiness to fulfill the penance imposed by the priest. If this readiness to make satisfaction is not present, something essential to the sacrament of Penance is wanting. But if, on the other hand, the penance imposed by the priest is not performed because one overlooks it or forgets about it, that does not invalidate the reception of the sacrament. Very often what the priest imposes on us as a penance in Confession may not be particularly difficult. But here it is not so much what we do that counts but, rather, the power of Christ, which is operative in sacramental satisfaction.

"This satisfaction that we make for our sins is not to such a degree ours that it is not made also through Christ Jesus [*neque ita nostra est satisfactio haec . . . ut non sit per Christum Jesum*]. In him we make satisfaction, bring forth 'fruits worthy of penance' (Lk 3: 8), which have their value from him, are offered to the Father by him and are accepted by the Father through him" (Council of Trent, Session XIV, ch. 8). He, our Savior, by means of the sacrament of Penance, infuses his own expiatory power into the works of penance imposed on us by the priest. He lays hold of our works of penance, as it were, and makes them his works of satisfaction and atonement. May we not be assured, then, that the temporal punishment due to our sins is remitted by the acceptance and performance of our sacramental penance?

But the power of this sacrament of Penance goes much further. It is a great consolation to know that the priest does not dismiss us until he has said over us the prayer *Passio Domini*: "May the Passion of our Lord Jesus Christ, the merits of the Blessed Virgin Mary and of all the saints, whatever good you have done and whatever evil you have suffered bring to you the remission of your sins, and increase of grace and the reward of eternal life. Amen." What treasures we have at our disposal in frequent Confession! What the priest imposes as sacramental satisfaction may well be something small. But the expiatory power of this small thing becomes united with the infinitely precious satisfaction of our suffering and dying Savior. Moreover it is joined to the prayers, sacrifices, good works, and sufferings of the Mother of God and of all the saints, and thereby its atoning power is increased anew. Finally, all the good we have done and all the suffering and adversity we have undergone is raised to the plane of sacramental satisfaction, which draws its value from Christ himself.

All these sufferings and adversities of ours come under the influence of the sacrament and of the power of Christ, which is working in the sacrament; they are made fruitful for us for the forgiveness of our sins, for the positive development of our life in Christ, and for the attainment of our final destiny in Heaven. Truly the generosity and helpfulness of our Mother, the Church, and the authority given to the priest in the sacrament of Penance, and the power of the sacrament itself are things unspeakably great. And the more frequently we receive this holy sacrament, which is so rich in graces, and the better we prepare ourselves for it, the more fully will its power be effective in us.

By means of frequent Confession, all our prayers and works and sufferings and our whole life become one big act of satisfaction for our sins, all animated and elevated by the atoning power of Christ! May we not then expect everything from God, even the remission of the temporal punishment due to our sins, even avoidance of the fire of Purgatory? And this all the more in proportion as we make better use of frequent Confession.

3. It is, unfortunately, a fact that very often we treat our sacramental penance in a very offhanded way, as if it were of no importance. It is true, of course, that in the practice of frequent Confession it is not through having penances imposed on us by the priest that our use of the sacrament is going to become more profitable for us. The growth of a spirit of penance in us must come about otherwise; it must come from the interior, from the one who receives the sacrament, not from the priest. If the performance of the penance imposed on us by the priest is really to have meaning and be fruitful and form a vital and organic part of the sacrament, it must proceed from a genuine desire to satisfy for sin and make atonement; it must be the outcome of a genuine spirit of penance. Such a spirit of penance is a natural attitude for us after we have sinned, especially as we come to recognize more and more what sin is and as we begin to understand God's holiness and his right to our self-surrender and love.

This spirit of penance means a continual, earnest, lively displeasure at the sins we have committed. It means that we are prepared to accept willingly the consequences of sin: the sufferings and troubles and hard things of life, whether they come directly from God or indirectly from him through the circumstances in which our lives are cast, through our fellow men. It means, in addition, that we freely impose some works of penance and satisfaction upon ourselves.

If this enduring spirit of penance is strong in us, then the penance imposed by the priest will be fruitful and will have meaning for us. And our frequent Confession will be more than a quickly performed, isolated act, more than merely another "religious exercise." It will lead to a practice of penance and atonement that will enrich our whole spiritual life and that will be of great significance for our spiritual development.

Frequent Confession will certainly nourish and deepen the spirit of penance in us and give us strength to face life's daily troubles and privations. It will help us to do our duty faithfully and conscientiously in all things, crucifying ourselves daily with our crucified Lord and allowing ourselves to be made victims for God, willing to be consumed for the honor and interests of God and of Christ, of the Church and of souls. And not merely that. We belong to the community of the Church. And we can make satisfaction to God for the sins of others also: what we call vicarious atonement. Here we have a test for our zeal for the interests of God and Christ, of the Church and of souls. Here our spirit of penance can show itself too.

Finally, we know that all our works of penance and atonement derive their value and their power from Christ—from the fact that they are united to the sufferings of Christ and his atoning sacrifice on the cross. The more we offer the sufferings of Christ to God the Father and, in union with Christ's sufferings and in the complete surrender of our will to the will of the Father, do the little that we can do, the more valuable and effective will be our penance and atonement. For as Christ himself said: "Without me you can do nothing" (Jn 15: 5).

O Lord, look down graciously on the holy zeal of thy
people and grant that we who mortify our bodies
may, through our good works, grow strong in spirit.
Amen.

CHAPTER NINETEEN

Sacramental Grace

1. Each of the sacraments of the New Testament produces, as its first effect, sanctifying grace. If the person who receives the sacrament is already, as we say, in the state of (sanctifying) grace, then the sacrament increases grace, produces "an increase of sanctifying grace."

This is the first and fundamental effect of Confession too. It gives an increase in grace, an increase in that new life we have from Christ and in Christ; an increase in purity of soul and light and strength, in holiness and union with God. It gives an increase in that new and higher mode of existing and living and knowing and willing that surpasses all merely natural and human life and existence as much as Heaven surpasses earth, that belongs to an altogether higher world full of divine nobility and splendor.

2. The life of grace! Natural, unredeemed man is on his own; he depends on himself. He has to rely on his own proud and egoistic interpretation of his experience and of the events of his life. He has to trust his own covetous self-seeking and his boundless self-centeredness and his hatred for everything that contradicts his own will. He is the unfortunate man of whom it is written: "To will is present with me, but to accomplish that which is good, I find not. For the good which I will, I do not; but the evil which I will not, that I do. . . . I find then a law, that when I have a will to do good, evil is present with me. . . . Unhappy man that I am!" (Rom

7: 18–24). What can bring help here? What is the remedy? Not nature, only grace. Now, in frequent Confession what is above all given to us is an increase of healing grace, what theologians call *gratia sanans.*

We may say that as a result of sin a threefold division has come into being for man; he has become divided from God, divided within himself, and divided from his fellow men. First of all, by sin man was cut off from God, divided from him; that was the first division, and it is the origin and cause of the other two. Men separated, detached from God, "became vain in their thoughts, and their foolish heart was darkened. . . . Wherefore God gave them up to the desires of their heart, unto uncleanness . . . to shameful affections. . . . And as they liked not to have God in their knowledge, God delivered them up to a reprobate sense, to do these things which are not convenient, being filled with all iniquity, malice . . . avarice, wickedness . . . inventors of evil things, foolish, without affection, without fidelity, without mercy" (Rom 1: 21–31). That is St. Paul's picture of mankind without God.

Secondly, by sin man was divided within himself; opposition arose between his higher and lower self. "When I have a will to do good, evil is present with me. For I am delighted with the law of God, according to the inward man. But I see another law in my members, fighting against the law of my mind and captivating me in the law of sin, that is in my members. Unhappy man that I am!" (Rom 7: 21–24).

Thirdly, by sin a division was introduced between man and man, between nation and nation. Hatred, enmity, ill-will, unkindness, envy, strife, jealousy, murder, war: that is the sad history of unredeemed man, of mankind without God, far away from God.

What can, what will repair this threefold division,

close these three clefts caused by sin? Grace and only grace. The cleft between God and man is closed by the grace of divine sonship, which was won for us by Christ through his death and which makes us children of the Father, "the elect of God, holy and beloved" (Col 3: 12).

The second cleft, in man himself, is closed only slowly and with difficulty, through the continual working of grace and self-discipline; that is to say, through the subjection and guidance of the lower powers and impulses to the control and guidance of the higher man, the man of grace and of union with God, the supernatural Christian man. Little by little, peace and the serene and harmonious order that preceded sin are reestablished within man's interior household—as the result of grace.

The third cleft, between man and man and between nation and nation, is closed too only by grace. All who have life from Christ, of whatever race or nation they be, live—in different degrees, it may be—one and the same supernatural life and drink from the same source, from "the one spirit," in whom "all have been made to drink" (1 Cor 12: 13) and who is given to them with sanctifying grace. This grace unites us all interiorly so that we all "may be one" (Jn 17: 21). But the unity it gives is not from common blood or from any short-lived, unenduring biological bond arising out of natural generation. First and foremost it is on the spiritual level, by means of the life that flows through our souls from Christ, that we participate in a really personal and enduring common life and in interior unity and brotherhood; on the spiritual level, where, in a supernatural but nevertheless real way, we are branches of the one true Vine, Christ, who communicates the fullness of his life to all of us; where the power of the one Holy Spirit governs and enlivens us—all through sanctifying grace.

Sanctifying grace is a healing grace, *gratia sanans*, that closes those three clefts caused by sin. It is at the same time an elevating grace, *gratia elevans*, that enriches and ennobles man interiorly and unites him to God. It lifts him up to the very purity and fullness and fecundity of the divine life itself. When sanctifying grace has taken possession of man's soul, then those consoling words of St. Paul are verified: "The charity of God is poured forth in our hearts, by the Holy Spirit who is given to us" (Rom 5: 5). And Christ himself tells us: "If any man love me, he will keep my word, and my Father will love him, and we will come to him, and will make our abode with him" (Jn 14: 23).

We have, indeed, fellowship "with the Father and with his Son, Jesus Christ" (1 Jn 1: 3); we share in the life of the great, holy, almighty God, who lives in us, Father, Son, and Holy Spirit. Now we are children of God, something infinitely greater than mere servants and bondsmen. Grace opens up for us the way to friendship and intimacy with God. God shows toward us the tenderness and attention that one shows toward a friend, and we may approach him with the ease and familiarity of a friend. So attractive is the beauty of grace that it overpowers the heart of God and causes it to be carried away with inexpressible love for us. God cannot do otherwise. He must love the soul in the state of grace with a divine love. And God's love is divinely strong and unconquerable. It is a love as a result of which he not only has us in view and is mindful of us but is indeed continually present to us and in us with his whole being, lovingly stooping down to us and giving himself to us. It is a love with which he so loves us, each one of us, just as if there were nothing else in the whole world for him to love; an inexhaustible, insatiable love that never grows weary of us as long as it finds that wonderful possession, grace, in us.

By means of grace, our soul becomes a clear mirror, showing forth the beauty of God, reflecting this beauty in all its purity and fullness. It becomes a temple of God, a throne of God, most wonderfully constructed and decorated by God himself. By means of grace we are "children of the light," "the light of the Lord" (Eph 5: 8), transfigured to the very depths of our souls with heavenly beauty and divine splendor. The eyes of our soul are illuminated with divine light—here and now in this world with the light of faith, which hereafter in Heaven will be replaced by the ineffable light of glory. Grace causes our souls to blossom forth like a magnificent garden that blooms in a perpetual springtime and knows no winter; that is always putting forth new blossoms without, however, letting the old ones wither; that charms the eye and heart of God with its splendor and profusion and on which God pours down his choicest blessings.

Along with grace all the supernatural virtues come into our souls, like richly adorned attendants following their noble queen—faith, hope, charity, justice, prudence, fortitude, and all the others, together with the gifts of the Holy Spirit and the various actual graces that are given us continually day by day in the form of enlightenment of spirit and stimulation of will—in all, spiritual wealth without equal. Well may we apply to sanctifying grace the words of the Book of Wisdom: "All good things come to me together with her and innumerable riches through her hands. . . . She is an infinite treasure to men, which they that use become the friends of God" (Wis 7: 11, 14).

An increase in sanctifying grace: that is what frequent Confession effects in us. But the other sacraments—Confirmation, Holy Communion, and the rest—also give an increase in sanctifying grace when they are received by one who is already in the state of grace. And yet the effect of Confirmation or Holy Communion is different from that of Confession. Sanctifying grace is one and the same always, but as given in the different sacraments it has a different mode and function, according to the nature of the particular sacrament in question. This different property or power, inherent in what is essentially the same sanctifying grace given in the different sacraments, is what we mean by "sacramental grace." It is sanctifying grace insofar as it is produced with this particular function and power by this particular sacrament and by it only—by Confirmation, for example, or by Holy Communion, or by the sacrament of Penance.

The sacramental grace that we receive in our frequent Confessions is an increase in sanctifying grace in such a way that this grace has as its special power and function the overcoming of those venial sins to which we have been prone in the past. It is true that venial sin can never destroy sanctifying grace in the soul, nor can it lessen it or deprive it of even one degree of its beauty. Nevertheless, venial sin stains, as it were, and sullies the brightness of sanctifying grace; it banks down grace's holy fire so that it can no longer burn freely and strongly; it weakens the ardor and the fecundity of grace, stifles its life-giving power, prevents its growth and its effectiveness.

Now, frequent Confession produces an increase in grace, and this grace has the special power to purify the soul from all stain so that grace can shine forth there once again in all its beauty and purity. It has the power to rid the soul, gradually, of everything that limits and confirms the ardor and the effectiveness of grace and that hinders the development of the interior life. It has the power to subject our natural energies fully to the actions of grace and to direct them toward the divine and supernatural. It has the power to fill us with the spirit of penance and with a lasting supernatural sorrow for the sins we have committed and thus to make us secure and strong for the future against sin and unfaithfulness. It enables us to strive effectively, through the power of Christ, against the causes and roots of our venial sin and against the evil tendencies they have developed in us. It gives the soul a new freshness and a new energy to arise and go forward. According to the opinion of many theologians, it gives us a title to all the actual graces—in the form of enlightenment and good inspirations and interior stimulation—that we need in order to reap the full fruit of frequent Confession.

Surely, then, frequent Confession should be something very dear and sacred to us! Ought we not make every effort to ensure that we benefit by it as much as possible?

> *Bless the Lord, O my soul, and never forget all he hath done for thee: who forgiveth all thy iniquities, who crowneth thee with mercy and compassion. For according to the height of the heaven above the earth, he hath strengthened his mercy toward them that fear him. As far as the east is from the west, so far hath he removed our iniquities from us.*
>
> —FROM PSALM 103

CHAPTER TWENTY

The Fear of God

Converse in fear during the time of your sojourning here.

— 1 PETER 1: 17

1. In our relationship with God, there are for us Christians two fundamental attitudes that are complementary to one another and that perfect one another: love and homage; intimacy and humble, submissive awe; nearness and distance. "I shudder, and my heart begins to glow at the same time," says St. Augustine. "I shudder because I am so unlike him: and my heart glows because I am so like him" *(Confessions* 11.9). And St. Bernard says with truth: "Holiness consists in a holy disposition of heart, a twofold disposition: a holy fear of God and a holy love of him. These are the two arms with which we embrace God" *(De consid.* 5.15). And the Church makes us pray: "Grant us, O Lord, that we may fear and at the same time love thy holy name always" (Collect, 2nd Sunday after Pentecost). We feel ourselves drawn to God, in whom is all goodness, all purity, everything that can make us happy and fulfill all our desires. And at the same time we have to bow down humbly before God, the supreme and absolute Being, the Lord of all, majestic and inaccessible. We have to keep our distance from him, show him respect and worship, adore him, submit our will to him, fear his judgments.

2. "The fear of the Lord is the beginning of wisdom," says the psalmist (Ps 111: 10). "The fear of the Lord is honor and glory," says Ecclesiasticus. "It shall delight the heart and shall give joy and gladness and length of days" (Sir 1: 11–12). And there is the promise: "The Lord will do the will of them that fear him: and he will hear their prayer and save them" (Ps 145: 19). Christ himself warns us: "And I say to you, my friends: Be not afraid of them who will kill the body and after that have no more that they can do. But I will show you whom you shall fear: Fear ye him who, after he hath killed, hath the power to cast into Hell. Yea, I say to you: Fear him" (Lk 12: 4–5).

When it is a question of overcoming sin and breaking away from it and sincerely amending our lives, then especially the fear of God has an important part to play. "Pierce thou my flesh with thy fear" (Ps 119: 120). We want a fear of God's holy and inexorable punitive justice, which is capable of destroying and wiping off the face of the earth whole societies and peoples and even entire civilizations on account of sin. We want a fear of God's justice, which did not spare the fallen angels, which on account of sin decreed so much misery and suffering for us men and made us all subject to death, the bitterest of the fruits of sin. We want a fear of God's justice as shown in Purgatory and especially in Hell, where it causes never-ending torments and wretchedness and eternal separation from God. Yes, O Lord, "pierce thou my flesh with thy fear." Let it take root so deeply in my soul that it may always restrain me, preserve me from evil, and incite me to carry on the struggle against sin.

The fear of God, however, is necessary not merely that we may turn away from sin. Even after we have turned completely to God and broken with mortal sin we still need to be penetrated with the fear of God. Fear of God impels us to do penance for the sins we have committed and preserves us from falling back into our sins and faults again. The thought of the punishment that we deserve for our sins helps us to face the daily difficulties and deprivation and struggles, without which there cannot be any real freedom from sin or any perfect union with God. We always have, indeed, plenty of reason to be penetrated with the fear of God when we consider the many occasions of sin all around us, our own extreme weakness, the strength of our inordinate attachments and habits, our natural inclination to self-indulgence, the pull of our own concupiscence from within and the attractions of the world from without, the many faults and defects and carelessnesses of which we are guilty every day.

Many people underestimate the importance of the fear of God on the ground that it seems to them too self-centered, too egoistic, something almost unworthy of a Christian. They think that nothing less than pure love of God is of any value. But this is quite a wrong attitude. It is true that the piety that is based on disinterested love must be placed above that arising from fear. But it would be an unhealthy exaggeration to regard the former as the only genuine piety.

The fear of which we are speaking here, let it be remembered, is not an absolute and entirely servile fear—what the theologians call *timor serviliter servilis,* "slavishly servile fear"—which concerns itself only with the punishment a certain course of action entails. The man who has such servile fear would sin boldly were it not for the punishment involved. His fear does not exclude the will to sin; it does not prevent his will being directed toward sin. It excludes only the carrying out of the sinful act, not the interior affection to sin.

The Fear of God

The fear of God that we are recommending is what is known as "simply servile fear" *(timor simpliciter servilis)*. It makes us fear God's displeasure and his punishments, but in such a way that it affects our will and turns us away from sin. The will does break with sin, even if it does so on account of the punishment that sin entails. This "simply servile fear" overcomes the will's attachment to sin. It is a morally good, noble, and salutary fear—though, of course, it falls very short of a filial fear of God. It is "a gift of God and an impulse of the Holy Spirit," as the Council of Trent expressly teaches (Session XIV, ch. 4). Filial fear, *timor filialis Dei*, is the fear that arises from perfect love of God, from filial love; it is most closely connected with this love, being at the same time its expression and its safeguard. Filial fear and filial love of God really go together to form one single disposition toward God, based on two diverse considerations. We look on God's goodness, and we are inflamed with love for him; we look on his majesty and on his justice and then on ourselves, and we are filled with fear lest through our sins we should lose him whom we love.

3. Fear is only "the beginning of wisdom," but it is the beginning; it is an indispensable foundation and a continual and powerful spur. "Blessed is the man that feareth the Lord" (Ps 112: 1). "The fear of the Lord hateth evil" (Prov 8: 13). It rouses us from our deceptive and dangerous sloth. The greatest evil, indeed, is not so much sin itself as sloth: remaining in sin, not taking thought, failing to reflect on ourselves. Fear is the greatest safeguard against our weakness. In general, it is above all fear that will protect us against future sin. Notwithstanding the great excellence of disinterested love in comparison with fear, in the long run there are relatively few who overcome all difficulties and avoid all

sin, including venial sin, from the motive of disinterested love alone. How true are the words of the *Imitation of Christ*: "If you wish to make progress, keep yourself in the fear of God and do not allow yourself too much liberty. . . . There is no true liberty, no genuine joy, except with the fear of God and a good conscience" (bk. I, ch. 21). "He who lays aside the fear of God will not be able to remain good for long, but will very quickly fall into the snares of the devil" (bk. I, ch. 24). The fear and the love of God must go together. If a person cultivates only the love of God, he stands in danger, like the Quietists, of falling into a presumptuous trust in God's goodness and, consequently, of growing careless in the struggle for perfection. If, on the other hand, one is motivated only by the fear of God's judgments, as were the Jansenists, then growth in the love of God is impossible. Indeed, even when we act habitually from very high and perfect motives, fear of God cannot be altogether excluded. It is present, even if entirely in the background, and fulfills an important function in our spiritual lives; it remains always the great safeguard against our moral weakness.

The motive of "simply servile fear" *(timor simpliciter servilis)* is an imperfect motive for loving God. We love God, but out of consideration for ourselves: because we fear the punishment that awaits us if we fail to love him and keep his Commandments. But this servile fear can and must lead us on to a filial fear, namely, to perfect love of God. Then it will produce in us a lively sense of the greatness and holiness of God and, along with this, a deep abhorrence of even the smallest sin. It will become the fear of a child who genuinely loves his father, and whose love makes it impossible for him to grieve his father or treat him badly. With this fear of grieving our loving and dearly beloved Father we shall be able, without great difficulty, to avoid sin and to lead lives pleasing to God. In this way, servile fear of God, no matter how self-centered and imperfect it is in itself, is seen to be an absolutely necessary starting point and a road leading to filial fear and perfect love of God.

4. When we come to Confession, it can often be very useful to us deliberately to base our contrition and our spirit of penance on the motive of the fear of God. We know that such contrition, what we call imperfect contrition, is in itself sufficient for the reception of the sacrament of Penance and even for the forgiveness of mortal sins that are confessed. But we will not content ourselves with this imperfect contrition; we will try to rise to filial fear, to the contrition of love, to contrition based on the motive of the perfect love of God. And thus the reception of the sacrament of Penance will be for us in truth a blessing.

In the interests of enlivening and improving our practice of frequent Confession as, indeed, in the interests of developing a sound Christian piety in our lives in general, it is important that, in a spirit of deep and lively faith, we keep continually before us those truths that foster in us a holy fear of God and allow them to influence us. Such truths are: our entire and absolute dependence on God; our sinfulness, our moral weakness, our daily failures notwithstanding all God's help and graces; God's inviolable holiness, purity, and justice and his judgments on sin in time and in eternity. Then there are the life and sufferings of Christ, which, more clearly than anything else, make us understand what God's holiness is and what sin means in his sight. It is in the very nature of things that God must be concerned about sin and must punish it: because he is holy, because he is holiness itself. He cannot be indifferent with regard to sin, no matter how small or trivial the sin may seem to us here in this world. And it is a fact too that Christ is not only the exalted and glorified Lord, seated on his Father's right hand in Heaven, but, first of all, the historical Christ, the humiliated, suffering Christ who hung on the cross in pain and ignominy to make satisfaction for our sins—for *my* sins.

Man's sin, indeed, is terrible in proportion as God's holiness and justice are great. Perhaps we Catholics today are inclined to be rather one-sided in our attitude toward Christ, to think too much of the glorified, exalted Christ and not pay sufficient attention to the suffering Christ who made satisfaction for our sins. This could only result in an inadequate concept of the holiness and justice of God, who punishes sin. It would impair the development in us of that holy fear of God which is the beginning of wisdom and the foundation for every truly religious and holy life. It would be to the detriment too of a full understanding of sin, including venial sin, of Confession, and of the practice of Penance. May God's grace graciously preserve us from all such one-sidedness!

Grant us, O Lord, always to fear and at the same time to love thy Holy Name; always to love thee, the all-holy God. For thou dost never withdraw thy care from those whom thou hast made secure in thy love. Amen.

CHAPTER TWENTY-ONE

Self-interested Love

For what have I in Heaven? And besides thee, what do I deserve upon earth? Thou art the God of my heart, and the God that is my portion for ever.
—PSALM 73: 25–26

1. Perfect love of God is a most noble and exalted thing. It means that we love God for his own sake, without any conscious or express reference to our own interests or our own temporal or eternal welfare. It is otherwise with what we call self-interested love of God. With it we love God, indeed, but for our own sake. We love him because we see that the happiness after which we are always and necessarily seeking is to be found in him and only in him and because we want to be sure of attaining it in him. We love him because he is our final end and our greatest good, both here and hereafter, and because in him is to be found our happiness and the complete fulfillment of all our wishes and desires.

This self-interested love of God is an imperfect love because it is love of God not for his sake but out of consideration for our own interests. It is imperfect and self-centered just like that love of God which arises from the fear of losing him and going to Hell. It is indeed a true and genuine love of God, but first and foremost it has in view our own salvation, which we hope for from God and which we know is to be found in him.

Thus, it is a selfish love of God—not in the sense that our ultimate aim is purely and solely our own happiness, which happens to be found in God, but in the sense that we really love God, admittedly insofar as he is the source of our happiness and our salvation both in time and eternity. The motive underlying this self-interested love is, of course, the hope of eternal salvation.

Is this self-interested, self-centered love of God morally unobjectionable, good, worthy of a Christian? Doesn't God deserve perfect love, love for his own sake and without regard to our own interests? Doesn't he demand such love? How is the self-interested love of which we have been speaking compatible with the command to love God with our whole heart and with our whole soul, that is, to love him with a perfect love?

There have been, in fact, not a few who have condemned as morally reprehensible and unlawful all self-interested love and love arising from the motive of the fear of punishment. And not only heretics, like Luther and Calvin, but also deeply religious and holy Catholics have held this view. There was, for example, Fénelon, archbishop of Cambrai at the end of the seventeenth century, with his doctrine of "disinterested love." According to Fénelon, the perfect soul loves God continually and uninterruptedly with a love so pure that every self-interested motive is excluded. Hence a person who has attained the perfection of the Christian life cannot any more make an act of hope of eternal life. Henceforth he must, rather, be indifferent regarding his eternal salvation. "Neither fear of punishment nor desire of reward has any place in such a state of perfection," says Fénelon. "God is no longer loved in order to acquire merit, nor for the sake of our own perfection, nor because our happiness is to be found in his love. Every 'interested motive' of fear and of hope disappears." These views, however, were rejected by the Church and expressly condemned as "pernicious and erroneous" in the brief of Pope Innocent XII, *Cum alias*, issued in 1699 (Denzinger, *Enchirid. Symb.*, nos. 1327–49). Nevertheless, even today we sometimes come across a certain tendency to look down on self-interested love as something inferior and to despise the efforts of pious souls who strive to advance in the interior life and grow in virtue and perfection in order that they may increase their merits for eternity. The implication is that the perfect Christian should strive after only a completely selfless love of God, a love with no element of legitimate self-interested love of God or of healthy, well-ordered, and morally good love of self. All self-love is regarded as something at least inordinate, if not sinful, and therefore unfit to serve even as a beginning, as a first step toward perfect and disinterested love of God.

2. According to the teaching of the Church, the virtue of hope, like the virtues of faith and charity, is a divine virtue. It has God for its immediate object—God inasmuch as he constitutes our eternal happiness. By means of the divine virtue of hope we confidently expect the good things promised us by God, especially our future happiness with him in Heaven, to be obtained by his grace and our own merits. We are, in the words of St. Paul, chosen to be "according to the faith of the elect of God and the acknowledging of the truth, which is according to godliness, unto the hope of life everlasting" (Titus 1: 1–2). And in another place the same Apostle prays (for the Ephesians) "that the God of our Lord Jesus Christ may give unto you the spirit of wisdom and of revelation, in the knowledge of him: the eyes of your heart enlightened, that you know what the hope is of his calling and what are the riches of the

glory of his inheritance in the saints [that is, in those who are baptized, Christians] and what is the exceeding greatness of his power toward us who believe" (Eph 1: 17–19). And again, to the Romans, he says: "Every creature groaneth and travaileth in pain . . . even we ourselves, waiting for the adoption of the sons of God, the redemption of our body" (Rom 8: 22–23). And "by him [Christ] we have access through faith into this grace wherein we stand: and glory in the hope of the glory of the sons of God" (Rom 5: 2).

Our hope must not be confined to eternal happiness alone but must extend also to many other objects insofar as these are helpful toward obtaining eternal happiness. We hope to get from God all the supernatural help and guidance and enlightenment and inspirations and graces that are necessary or useful for us in attaining our eternal salvation. We hope to get from him all the help we need in our work, our various struggles, our sufferings, and our difficulties; so that we may stand steadfast in temptation, repent of our sins, practice the Christian virtues, and thus lead a holy life. Christ our Lord came on earth, after all, that we might "have life and have it more abundantly" (Jn 10: 10). We may hope even for temporal things from God, insofar as they are either necessary or helpful as a means to our salvation, for example, a long life, health, worldly possessions, the respect and esteem of our fellow men.

Does not our Lord himself promise that those who leave house, brethren, sisters, and father and mother for his name's sake "shall receive a hundredfold and shall possess life everlasting" (Mt 19: 29)? To those who work in his vineyard he promises and, at the end of the day, gives their hire (Mt 20: 1–9). To the poor in spirit he promises the Kingdom of Heaven. To those who hunger and thirst after justice he promises that they will have their fill. To the clean of heart he promises that they will see God. "Blessed are ye," he said, "when they shall revile and persecute you for my sake. Be glad and rejoice, for your reward is very great in Heaven" (Mt 5: 11–12). All these motives to which our Lord refers are self-interested ones. Let it be noted too that the Church's liturgy again and again tries to encourage us to fight on as Christians, denying ourselves and sparing no effort, by appealing to well-ordered self-love and to self-interested love of God.

Finally, it is clear that if we endeavor to cultivate only a completely unselfish love of God and fail to develop together with it a legitimate self-interested love of God and a healthy and well-ordered self-love, then we shall fall into a very one-sided spirituality. The lower powers of the soul will remain entirely unsatisfied. Indeed, it might mean that they would be suppressed by violence and that some of the fundamental tendencies of our soul, such as our natural desire for happiness, would never be morally purified or ennobled. And the result would be that, with such one-sided piety and over-spiritualized love of God, we should never develop strong human characters or become vigorous Christian and religious personalities. Rather, we should belong to that "pious" type who make little impression on others or who, indeed, sometimes even repel others.

God has made us in such a way that by nature we are moved for the most part by what affects our own well-being. For this reason Christ set before us our love of ourselves as the norm for Christian charity toward our neighbor, and the law holds good everywhere that well-ordered charity begins with charity toward ourselves. My own sanctification and perfection come before that of others and, consequently, well-ordered self-love is part of the practice of virtue, so much so that it is impossible to exclude all self-love or to be indifferent regarding one's true happiness.

At the same time self-love must not be the final thing; our own interests must not be our sole and ultimate aim. It would be a disordered and perverse self-love that would regard God merely as a means to our own happiness and love him only for that reason. Self-love is for us, necessarily, nothing but a way to a higher love; it leads us above itself to the perfect love of God. And this from the moment at which we begin to love ourselves for the love of God because, and insofar as, we are God's creatures, God's children, the instruments of his glorification. Thus, love for God becomes the motive of our own love of self: we love ourselves in God, for God's sake. We love everything that belongs to God, and therefore we love ourselves, because we ourselves belong to God too.

In this way self-love leads us above itself—up to the perfect love of God—because we now see that more than our mere self is concerned in our own eternal salvation. We see that God's honor and glory enters in too because, in actual fact, our eternal happiness consists in knowing and loving God and in adoring, thanking, praising, and glorifying him, in and through Christ, our glorified Lord, in and with the Church and with the angels and saints.

3. From what we have said it will be clear that it is a lawful and well-founded practice to make use of self-interested love as a motive of contrition when going to Confession. This contrition will not be perfect contrition; nevertheless, in Confession it will suffice to obtain pardon from God, even for mortal sins. We ought, however, always—and especially when we are preparing for Confession—try to use this self-interested love, this desire for the possession of God and the happiness that it

brings, only as a way that will lead us up to perfect love for God: to that love by which we love ourselves in God as his creatures and children, as the instruments of his glorification, which in our own happiness we seek and intend; to that love which will cause us to long to make our lives both here on earth and hereafter in Heaven one long act of adoration and glorification of God, one holy and unceasing song of praise to God, Father, Son, and Holy Spirit.

> *O almighty and eternal God, grant us an increase of faith, hope, and charity; and that we may deserve to obtain what thou dost promise, make us love what thou commandest. Amen.*
> —COLLECT, 13TH SUNDAY AFTER PENTECOST

CHAPTER TWENTY-TWO

Perfect Love

Perfect charity casteth out fear.

—1 JOHN 4: 18

1. The very essence and, at the same time, the zenith of Christian piety consists in the perfect love of God. It is the love of God *for his own sake,* that is, because he is infinitely good in himself and worthy of all our love, because he is the fullness of all purity and nobility, of goodness, holiness, and greatness.

Of this perfect love of God St. Paul wrote: "If I speak with the tongues of men and of angels and have not charity, I am become as sounding brass or a tinkling cymbal. And if I should have prophecy and should know all mysteries and all knowledge, and if I should have all faith, that I could remove mountains, and have not charity, I am nothing. And if I should distribute all my goods to feed the poor, and if I should deliver my body to be burned, and have not charity, it profiteth me nothing" (1 Cor 13: 1–3). St. Paul is not referring here to any natural, spontaneous, sensible love, to any purely instinctive impulse. Nor does he mean a purely natural, rational, or spiritual love based on clear knowledge and a firm act of the will. He is speaking of a supernatural love, founded on faith and grace, that is directed to God and to all creatures out of regard for God and for his sake.

This perfect love is a "divine" virtue. It is called "divine" charity because it has God for its immediate object and because everything it embraces outside God is embraced out of regard for God, for his sake and in him. It is called "divine" charity also because it is "poured forth in our hearts by the Holy Spirit" (Rom 5: 5), that is, because it is infused into our souls by God and cannot be acquired by our own efforts. Finally, it is "divine" charity because by means of it we are enabled to love God as only he himself, by virtue of his divine nature, can. It is a fire kindled in us by God himself, by the Holy Spirit dwelling in us with his divine love; an image and reflection of that divine mutual outpouring of love of the Father and the Son from which the Holy Spirit proceeds and which, indeed, is the Holy Spirit himself. It is a spark, a flame, of that divine love with which God himself burns. It is a rare blossom of divine life and divine blessedness.

Love is the sweetest and most delectable thing that exists in Heaven or on earth. Our heart has been made for love and in it finds its happiness. In love it opens up its innermost and deepest secrets in order to surrender itself to love and in it to live and flourish. Our heart desires nothing more than to find a worthy object for its love on which it can pour itself forth entirely. What a wonderful thing then is this divine, holy, supernatural love that is poured forth in our hearts along with sanctifying grace by the Holy Spirit, which comes directly from God and has God for its object!

The *Imitation of Christ* is quite right when it says: "There is nothing sweeter than love, nothing stronger, nothing higher, nothing more comprehensive, nothing more delightful, nothing fuller or better, in Heaven or on earth: because love is born of God and can find rest only above all created things, in God alone. He that loves, flies, runs, and is full of joy; he is free and not held back. He gives all for all and has always all things: because he rests in One alone, who is most high above all and from whom all good comes" (bk. 3, ch. 5). It is this divine, holy, supernatural love, and it alone, that rises up to God with a holy audacity, with the simplicity of a child and the familiarity of a bride, and clasps him in the sweetest and most intimate embrace, penetrates into the innermost recesses of his goodness and sweetness and dissolves in the depths of his divine heart.

It is only through this holy love that we can truly possess God as our own. By means of it we possess him, not merely in wish and desire, but in the most perfect reality. Through love we have him, Almighty God, Father, Son, and Holy Spirit, in our hearts. Through it we approach nearer and nearer to him and grow more and more like him; our souls become unified to him and our minds, as it were, blended into his, just as when two flames unite together to form one. The divine nature is indeed a pure fire and a glowing torrent of love. If there is in us a similar fire of love, then this will unite itself to the former so intimately that their union is closer than any union of love among creatures and surpasses all earthly love as much as Heaven surpasses earth. The divine love and it alone can fully satisfy our heart with its torrent of divine bliss. It fills us with eternal and perpetually renewed life and inflames us with a heavenly fire. Christian hope is something very great, indeed. But, greater than even faith or hope is love. "Now there remaineth faith, hope, and charity, these three: but the greatest of these is charity (1 Cor 13: 13).

2. "Follow after charity" (1 Cor 14: 1). Charity, love of God, is the ultimate aim of all God's commandments. They can all be summed up in the one command:

"Thou shalt love the Lord, thy God." All other commands refer to that one, and by fulfilling it we fulfill them all. Every true fulfillment of duty is a work of love. For love is the first and last of all the virtues. "Charity is patient, is kind; charity envieth not, dealeth not perversely, is not puffed up, is not ambitious, seeketh not her own, is not provoked to anger, thinketh no evil; rejoiceth not in iniquity, but rejoiceth with the truth; beareth all things, believeth all things, hopeth all things, endureth all things" (1 Cor 13: 4–7). Charity includes every virtue. Where there is charity, there is all; and where charity is missing, all is missing.

That is why we are called to the practice of charity. "Thou shalt love the Lord, thy God." "O Lord," we pray, "enkindle in us thy love." "O Heart of Jesus, burning with love for us, inflame our hearts with love for thee." Now, it is by good works that love is nourished and developed. Love soon withers away and dies if it is not sustained by good works, just as a fire goes out if fuel is not supplied to it. The fuel is turned into flame by the fire, and then the fire is nourished and increased by the flame. In the same way our good works get their ardor from our love, and through the ardor of our good works our love is sustained and its fire increased. If we want to do good works, we must foster love, and if we want to have love, we must do good works. If we want to have perfect love, we must strive with all our power to increase in love by being unwearied in the performance of good works; we must be ready to do all the good that is possible for us in our circumstances.

3. "Follow after charity." Charity is the goal we are aiming at in Confession too. For freedom from sin is, after all, only a road or a gateway leading to the perfect love of God.

And here let us recall once more the harm venial sin does to the soul. It weakens the fervor of love, that big-hearted, courageous disposition that is ready to give everything to God, to sacrifice everything for him. Where there is venial sin the ardor and vigor of love can no longer develop. Instead, the growth of love is retarded, and its Godward tendency is checked and hindered. What immeasurable harm is this not merely for ourselves but also for the whole community, for the Church, and especially for the glory of God! How are we to overcome venial sin? Precisely by striving after love with the whole force of our will and by trying always to increase our love.

> *O Lord Jesus Christ, who hast said: Ask and it shall be given you, seek and you shall find, knock and it shall be opened to you: we beseech thee to make thy divine love burn within us so that in word and in deed we may love thee with our whole hearts and never cease to praise thee.*

CHAPTER TWENTY-THREE

The Love of Christ

Christ died for all: that they also who live may not live to themselves, but unto him who died for them and rose again.

—2 CORINTHIANS 5: 15

1. "Thou shalt love the Lord thy God with thy whole heart and with thy whole soul and with thy whole mind. This is the greatest and the first commandment" (Mt 22: 37–38). To love God, the Almighty God, Father, Son, and Holy Spirit: that is what we are commanded to do. Out of love God the Father sent us his only-begotten Son. Full of gratitude we acknowledge "the one Lord Jesus Christ, the only-begotten Son of God, born of the Father before all ages: God of God, Light of Light, true God of true God; begotten, not made, consubstantial with the Father" (Nicene Creed). To him, the Son of God, is due our entire and undivided love, all that love which we have for God himself. That great commandment, "Thou shalt love the Lord, thy God," binds us with regard to him too. To him, the incarnate Son of God, we must offer the fulness of love, just as we offer it to the Father and to the Holy Spirit: the love of gratitude, of complacency, of benevolence, of conformity to his will, of friendship. We must love him with our whole heart and with our whole soul and with all our strength. We must love him above all else and more

than everything else; and we must love everything else only for love of him. We must love him with an ardent, burning love that will dare all and sacrifice all and risk all for the Beloved.

2. (a) First of all, we owe Christ a great *love of gratitude* in return for all he has done for us. "For us men and for our salvation he came down from Heaven and was made flesh [took human nature] and became man." He was "in the form of God"; for he is God, true God. But "He emptied himself, taking the form of a servant, being made in the likeness of men and in habit found as a man. He humbled himself, becoming obedient unto death, even to the death of the cross" (Phil 2: 6–8). We think of Bethlehem, the crib, the stable, and the poverty of it all. We think of the flight into Egypt, the hidden life in Nazareth with its prayer and work and obedience to Mary and to Joseph. We think of his public life with all the difficulties, hardship, and privations that it entailed. We remember how he was hated, slandered, and defamed. We remember the Garden of Gethsemane and his scourging at the pillar and the condemnation by the Sanhedrin and by Pilate. We remember the crowning with thorns and the journey to Calvary and the cross on which he shed his blood. And all this was out of love for us men; out of love for me, personally! "He loved me and delivered himself for me" (Gal 2: 20). He had me clearly before his eyes. He thought of me in Bethlehem, in Nazareth, in Gethsemane, on Calvary. What great love! Must I not give him my entire love, an ardent, strong, rapturous, grateful love? "That they also who live may not now live to themselves, but unto him who died for them."

But Christ has done still more for us. He has ascended into Heaven, to his Father, and yet his love is so great that he cannot leave us. He wants to be near us, and so he has given himself to us in a new form and in a new kind of presence in the most holy sacrament of the Eucharist, the sacrament of love. "Having loved his own . . . he loved them unto the end" (Jn 13: 1) and gave them the greatest possible proof of his love: his own continual presence with them. He cannot do without us.

And so he spends his life worshipping and adoring the Father for us in our place; thanking him, offering satisfaction to him for our sins, interceding with him for us, his brethren. He is in our midst, thinking of us— of me—day and night, always. He is always concerned about us because of his great love for us. Day after day he offers himself in sacrifice as a victim to the Father, as a victim of praise and thanksgiving and atonement. He unites us with him in his sacrifice in order that with him and through him we may adore and honor the Father perfectly; in order that we may be true adorers adoring the Father in spirit and in truth: "for the Father seeketh such to adore him" (Jn 4: 23); in order that by taking part in the most holy sacrifice of the Eucharist we may share in the fruits and graces of the sacrifice of Calvary. His graces flow to us from the altar (of the Cross) in seven streams—the seven sacraments; and especially in Holy Communion, in which he himself with incomparable love becomes the food of our souls, a food that transforms us into him and fills us with his spirit and animates us with his life.

When we receive him in Holy Communion he rests within us, heart to heart, and allows us to taste the fullness of his sweetness and love. What great love! Must I not respond by returning to him the most tender and sincere love? And then his love in the other sacraments: in Baptism, Confession, Penance, the Anointing of the Sick! Truly, indeed, "He loved me and delivered himself for me" (Gal 2: 20). Surely I must love him in return with a great love of gratitude!

(b) And then there is the *love of conformity to his holy will.* Christ has become for us "the way and the truth and the life" (Jn 14: 6). He went along before us on the way we have to travel. He has made his holy will known to us in his exhortations, his instructions, and his commandments: Blessed, he said, are the poor in spirit, they that mourn, the meek, the clean of heart, the merciful (Mt 5: 3–8). These "beatitudes," as we call them, are so many guiding principles, not to say commands, for us. Christ taught us to pray: "Our Father who art in heaven. Hallowed be thy name . . . thy will be done. . . . Forgive us our trespasses as we forgive them who trespass against us" (cf. Mt 6: 9–13). He told us: "Be you perfect, as also your heavenly Father is perfect: who maketh his sun to rise upon the good and bad and raineth upon the just and the unjust. Love your enemies, do good to them that hate you and pray for them that persecute and calumniate you: that you may be the children of your Father who is in Heaven" (Mt 5: 44–48).

One thing above all was dear to his heart: that we should love one another as he loves us, that we should be one in love (Jn 13: 34; 15: 17; 17: 21). He entreats us, orders us: "Abide in my love. If you keep my commandments, you shall abide in my love: as I also have kept my Father's commandments and do abide in his love" (Jn 15: 9–10). In all these things where Christ's will has been manifested, we must show our love for him by conforming our will to his, by trying to carry out what he suggests to us or wishes from us or commands us to do. This is the love of deeds, as opposed to that of words; this is genuine, sincere, efficacious love for Christ.

We can learn Christ's holy will from his own manner of life and behavior, as depicted for us in the Gospels.

And we can learn it too from the inexhaustible mysteries of his life, which the Church's liturgy sets before us
year after year with the purpose of deepening our understanding of them and teaching us what he wants
from us. "Learn of me," he himself said (Mt 11: 29). "I
have given you an example, that as I have done to you,
so you do also" (Jn 13: 15). "If any man will come after
me, let him deny himself and takes up his cross and
follow me" (Mt 16: 24). He goes before us and calls to
us: "Come, follow me" (Mt 19: 21).

We must try to follow him with self-surrendering,
trustful love; with a love that gladly makes sacrifices for
his sake and that urges us to imitate him in all things—
both in our interior attitude toward the Father, toward
our fellow men, toward ourselves, and toward life in
general, and also in our exterior actions and behavior.
In joyous love we must try to share his life. With him we
must undertake a life of voluntary self-denial, abnega-
tion, and poverty; a life of humility, obedience, and
chastity; a life of renunciation of all that displeases God;
a life of adoration of God; a life of dull obscurity and
silence, prayer and work, and suffering in all its forms.
For love of him we must strive above all that our will,
our actions, and our whole life may be conformed entirely to his holy will and to his teaching and example.
This, indeed, is genuine and true love of Christ.

(c) With the *love of complacency* we rejoice at all the
power and glory the Father conferred on Christ, his divine Son made man. We rejoice at the fullness of wisdom and grace the Father poured forth on the human
nature of Christ; at the fullness of virtue that distin-
guished him from all other men; at the power the Father bestowed on him, the Son of Man, when he took
him up into Heaven and made him Lord and King of
all.

"Thou alone art holy; Thou alone art Lord; Thou alone, O Jesus Christ, art most high, together with the Holy Spirit, in the glory of God the Father" *(Gloria in excelsis)*. Must not Christ be our sole delight and rapture? When we look into his Sacred Heart, with perhaps the Litany of the Sacred Heart or of the Holy Name before us, and ponder over his excellence and glory, can we do anything else but rejoice and congratulate him with the most ardent love of complacency?

(d) And when we think of our humiliated Lord, rejected by so many, our love of complacency will become a *love of compassion*, a sympathetic love. It will make us lovingly contemplate the Passion of our Lord, as narrated for us in the Gospels. It will make us accompany him during all the stages of his Passion and through all the scenes of his suffering until we take our stand beside Mary and St. John at the foot of the cross. It will make us penetrate ever more deeply into the mystery of the love and sufferings of Christ. It will make us relive with him all the outrages and insults and torments that he went through, and it will make us die with him again out of love. It will make us be aware, with deep sorrow, how still today our Lord is rejected and cast out by mankind and branded as an impostor—in his own Person and in his Church, in his priests, and in his faithful ones. It will urge us to beg pardon and mercy from the Lord with all our power, to make atonement to him, to console him by greater loyalty and devotedness, just as the angel from Heaven consoled him in his hour of need in Gethsemane.

This love of compassion will give us strength to make the greatest sacrifices and renunciations and to share magnanimously in the sufferings of our loved Lord in order to comfort him and make him feel somewhat less all the bad treatment he receives from mankind. How fruitful, how precious is this sympathetic love! It is the love that our Blessed Lady offered him as she followed him along the way to Calvary.

(e) Finally, there is the *love of benevolence*. What do we wish for him, the beloved of our hearts? That he may be known and loved: in his Person, in his teaching, in his mysteries, in his Church, in his brethren. "The charity of Christ urges us on." And so we become apostles of prayer and lift up our hands day and night to beg for God's graces and blessings for the Church, for our Holy Father the Pope, for bishops and priests, and for all Christians. We burn with holy zeal for the souls that our Lord has purchased with his precious blood: that they may be rescued from the clutches of Satan and the allurements of the world, that they may find the way to Christ and, through him, to the Father. "The charity of Christ urges us on" to live ever more fully and entirely for him who died and rose from the dead for us; to honor him in all our actions and in every detail of our lives; to be worthy representatives of him before the world and in our own family circle and in our profession; to be everywhere and always living witnesses unto Christ through our own really Christian lives lived in imitation of him, our poor, humiliated, obedient, crucified Lord.

3. By means of frequent Confession we strive to attain that purity of heart which will set us free for the ardent love of Christ and make us rejoice in sacrifices for his sake; that purity of heart which will enable us to say with St. Paul: "The things that were gain to me, the same I have counted loss for Christ. Furthermore, I count all things to be but loss for the excellent knowledge of Jesus Christ, my Lord: for whom I have suffered the loss of all things and count them but as dung, that I may gain Christ and may be found in him; that I may

know him and the power of his resurrection and the fellowship of his sufferings, being made conformable to his death, if by any means I may attain to the resurrection which is from the dead" (Phil 3: 7–11).

Here on earth love involves suffering. True love for God and for Christ is generated by suffering and is developed and brought to perfection only beneath the shadow of the cross. He who is not willing to suffer does not love. Love urges us on to suffering because it is in suffering that it can reveal its full strength. And love must thus reveal itself, from an inner necessity. Above all, it is the love of our Savior, of our crucified Beloved, that urges us on to suffering. The contemplation of his Passion never fails to awaken a desire of suffering and atonement in a loving heart.

> *O Jesus Christ, most pure lover of my soul, lord of all creation! Who will give me the wings of true liberty, that I may fly to thee and find my rest in thee! When shall I become so fully rapt in thee that, through love of thee, I may cease to be aware of my own being and be aware only of thee? Come, oh come, for without thee no day or hour can be happy: for thou art my joy. Wretched am I and, as it were, imprisoned and loaded with fetters until thou refresh me with the light of thy presence and give me freedom and let me look on thy loving countenance.*
> —*Imitation of Christ*, BK. 3, CH. 21

CHAPTER TWENTY-FOUR

Fraternal Charity

"A new commandment I give unto you: that you love one another, as I have loved you."
—JOHN 13: 34

1. "Having loved his own who were in the world, he loved them unto the end. And when supper was done he riseth and layeth aside his garments and, having taken a towel, girded himself. After that, he putteth water into a basin and began to wash the feet of his disciples" (Jn 13: 1–5). It is the first demonstration on this evening of our Lord's meek and humble love for his disciples. And it is soon followed by a second. For, very shortly afterward, "taking bread, he gave thanks and broke and gave to them, saying: This is my body, which is given for you. Do this for a commemoration of me. In like manner, the chalice also, after he had supped, saying: This is the chalice, the new testament in my blood, which shall be shed for you" (Lk 22: 19–20).

Could he have given us anything more than he gave us when he instituted the Blessed Eucharist and left us the Holy Sacrifice of the Mass and invited us to partake of Holy Communion? Truly, indeed, he loved us unto the end, unto the limits of love. And he set the seal on that love the following day, Good Friday. "Greater love than this no man hath, that a man lay down his life for his friends" (Jn 15: 13). It was for this same reason that our Lord went to Gethsemane and allowed himself to be taken by his enemies and condemned and most shamefully scourged and crowned with thorns and put to death on the cross. It was all out of love for us: to make atonement for our guilt and win his Father's favor for us, so that he (the Father) would adopt us as his beloved children and bestow his love upon us.

When the time to bid farewell to his disciples was at hand Christ bequeathed to them, his own, along with the legacy of his flesh and blood, the legacy of his heart, a legacy of love. "A new commandment I give unto you: that you love one another, as I have loved you" (Jn 13: 34). His love for us is to be the measure and standard of the love we have for one another. And how does he love us? "As the Father hath loved me, I also have loved you" (Jn 15: 9). Where can there be a love more noble and sublime than that with which the Eternal Father loves his divine Son? With an equally noble and sublime love Christ loves us and gives us his commandment: that we love one another with that love with which he loves us.

Christ also gave a specific sign by which his followers could be recognized. It is not sensible consolation or transports of fervor in prayer. It is not any extraordinary activity or any extraordinary state of soul. It is not the power to work miracles. It is not any unusual graces of feelings or thoughts. It is love for our neighbor. "By this shall all men know that you are my disciples, if you have love one for another" (Jn 13: 35). That is the great commandment: "Thou shalt love the Lord thy God with thy whole heart. . . . This is the greatest and the first commandment. And the second is like to this: Thou shalt love thy neighbor as thyself" (Mt 22: 37–39).

2. Love of one's neighbor, as understood by Christ and by Christians, is not merely natural love. It is not a

love with which we love our fellow man on account of his natural qualities: because he is a good man, because he is of attractive character, because we get on well with him, and so forth. That would be loving our neighbor for the sake of man: for the sake of the man we encounter in him. Such a love may be noble, indeed, very noble; but it is not Christian charity. For Christian charity is a supernatural love, by means of which we love God in our neighbor. With it we love our neighbor for the sake of God and with the same love with which we love God and Christ. True Christian love of our neighbor is really love of God. In our neighbor we love God: we see him as God's creature, endowed with God's gifts and graces, God's child, the brother of Christ, a member of Christ, indeed, Christ himself. "As long as you did it to one of these my least brethren, you did it to me. I was hungry and you gave me to eat; I was thirsty and you gave me to drink. . . . Amen, I say to you, as long as you did it to one of these my least brethren, you did it to me" (Mt 25: 35–40).

We remember Saul as he drew near to Damascus long ago. "He had obtained from the authorities in Jerusalem the necessary documents authorizing him to bring bound to Jerusalem any followers of Christ on whom he could lay hands. As he approached Damascus, a light from Heaven suddenly shone around him, and he fell to the ground and heard a voice saying to him: 'Saul, Saul, why persecutest thou me?' And he asked: 'Who art thou, Lord?' And the answer came: 'I am Jesus whom thou persecutest'" (Acts 9: 2–5).

Christian charity toward the neighbor springs from a supernatural faith that sees in man something more than a mere creature of flesh and blood. Where there is no supernatural faith there can be no real Christian charity. Where there is little faith, there will be a want of

Christian charity too. Christian charity is ultimately nothing else but the extension to our neighbor of our love of God. The most certain foundation and the basic motive for love of our neighbor is God himself. Our supernatural love is directed first and foremost toward God, next and secondly toward our neighbor. But it is one and the selfsame supernatural love. And consequently our love for God is exactly as deep and extensive and strong as our love for our neighbor. "If any man say: I love God, and hateth his brother: he is a liar. For he that loveth not his brother whom he seeth, how can he love God whom he seeth not? And this commandment we have from God, that he who loveth God love also his brother" (1 Jn 4: 20–21).

Thus, the love of our neighbor is most closely connected with the love of God and the command to love our neighbor with the command to love God. So closely, indeed, are they connected that St. John does not hesitate to ascribe to the practice of fraternal charity the same effects that he ascribes to the practice of the love of God: "We know," he writes, "that we passed from death [the death of sin] to life [the life of grace and divine sonship], because we love the brethren. He that loveth not abideth in death [the death of sin]" (1 Jn 3: 14). And St. Paul has in mind both love of God and love of neighbor when he sings the canticle of love in his letter to the Corinthians: "If I speak with the tongues of men and angels, and have not charity, I am become as sounding brass, or a tinkling cymbal. And if I should have prophecy and should know all mysteries and all knowledge . . . I am nothing" (1 Cor 13: 1ff.). The love of God and of our neighbor are, indeed, one and the selfsame love.

Christian fraternal charity is a love of complacency with regard to all the natural and supernatural gifts and endowments that God's goodness has bestowed and continues to bestow upon our fellow men. We are gladdened and rejoiced at all these proofs of God's love, and we congratulate our neighbor who is the recipient of them. It is, too, to a large extent, a love of compassion, which makes us suffer with our neighbor in his infirmities and failures, which causes us to be genuinely afflicted on his account when we see him ensnared by sin and threatened with a terrible eternity if he does not amend his ways.

Christian love of our neighbor is also a love of benevolence toward him. We wish him, in the first place, everything that will advance the interests of his supernatural life: the grace of God, forgiveness of his sins, all the actual graces he needs, supernatural inspirations and enlightenment, strength to do good, the grace of final perseverance and eternal salvation. In the second place we wish him all those temporal goods and possessions that will help in any way in the attainment of his eternal destiny.

Christian love of our neighbor is a love that is active, that expresses itself in deeds. It makes us try genuinely never to be uncharitable in any way, either interiorly in thought or exteriorly in word, deed, or omission. It expresses itself in deeds and does everything it possibly can, as far as circumstances allow, to help our fellow men in a positive way. St. Pius X said very truly: "It must be firmly maintained that there is no more effective means of forming all in the likeness of Christ than charity." Charity opens up hearts and gives us power over them. There is no other language that the human heart understands so well as the language of love. We have no better way of winning over our neighbor to the service of God and of Christ than by the practice of genuine practical charity toward him.

3. How can we discover, without much difficulty and with full certainty, whether we are deriving profit from our Confessions? By asking ourselves whether we are becoming ever more concerned about the fulfillment of the precept of fraternal charity. To practice frequent Confession and at the same time to be wanting in the practice of charity to the neighbor, to be careless and without any supernatural zeal for the spiritual welfare of our fellow men, frequently and deliberately to speak and act uncharitably and to be impatient and severe and unkind toward others—these are things that are not reconcilable with one another.

In our practice of frequent Confession we must endeavor above all to understand and live up to the commandment to love God and to love our neighbor, including even our enemies. We have here a means of checking the state of our interior life and our love for God and for Christ. We need only ask ourselves whether we have a genuine intention of being charitable and whether we honestly strive to practice charity. We shall certainly fall into faults of frailty with regard to charity, but we must never on that account give up the struggle to go forward and gain the mastery over all the human weaknesses that are our lot. And especially it must be our concern that, no matter what the cost, we are never guilty of a deliberate and cold-blooded offense against charity.

In our examination of conscience for Confession and in our nightly examination as well, we must keep an eye particularly on our efforts to develop a charitable disposition and to act accordingly. Our purpose of amendment, too, should consist to a large extent in resolving to show charity to others, to put up with things out of charity, and to forgive in charity. "Let love be without dissimulation . . . loving one another with the charity of brotherhood, with honor preventing one another, in carefulness, not slothful, in spirit fervent . . . rejoicing in hope, patient in tribulation . . . communicating to the necessities of the saints [Christians]. . . . Bless them that persecute you: bless and curse not. Rejoice with them that rejoice; weep with them that weep; being of one mind one toward another; not minding high things, but consenting to the humble . . . to no man rendering evil for evil; providing good things . . . in the sight of all men. If it be possible as much as is in you, have peace with all men. Revenge not yourselves, my dearly beloved, but give place unto wrath. Be not overcome by evil: but overcome evil by good" (Rom 12: 9–21). "Charity is patient, is kind; charity envieth not, dealeth not perversely, is not puffed up, is not ambitious, seeketh not her own, is not provoked to anger, thinketh no evil, rejoiceth not in iniquity, but rejoiceth with the truth; beareth all things, believeth all things, hopeth all things, endureth all things" (1 Cor 13: 4–7).

These texts are mere pointers that suggest plenty of matter for our examination of conscience and for our purpose of amendment. And if we ever sin deliberately against charity or deliberately fail to show to others the charity we should, we must try to excite ourselves to an earnest and heartfelt sorrow, to a sorrow that will fill our souls and make us resolve with all the strength of our will to fashion our life into a life of charity.

If we make our Confessions in this earnest way, we may rest assured that they will be fruitful and will be blessed by God.

Grant, O Lord, that the grace of the Holy Spirit may enlighten our hearts and refresh them abundantly with the joys of perfect charity. Amen.

CHAPTER TWENTY-FIVE

The Life of Prayer

Another characteristic fruit that frequent Confession should produce is a deep and constant spirit of prayer in our lives.

1. The prayer of Christ, our High Priest, continually present in the Blessed Sacrament on our altars, is indeed something truly wondrous! Unceasingly, never wearying, day and night he prays, loves, gives thanks, adores, makes petition, and offers satisfaction. So pure, so holy, so sincere, so infinitely precious is the prayer he prays that the Father beholds this Suppliant with infinite gratification and accepts his prayer with divine good pleasure.

Our prayer is frequently interrupted by our work, by our conversation with others, by the various distractions and demands of daily life. It is a prayer that is often cold, lacking in fervor and attention, irreverent, hurried and superficial. We are conscious of the great difference there is between our prayer and Christ's prayer, and, therefore, from the depths of our misery we cry out earnestly to our Savior: "Lord, teach us to pray" (Lk 11: 1).

Who should make this request more sincerely, in his heart and with his lips, than he who practices frequent Confession and strives earnestly to lead a good life? And who is more likely to acquire a share of the grace of prayer than he who tries with all fervor to free himself from every deliberate fault, from imperfections, and from all inordinate inclinations to things and to persons, to free himself above all from himself? This, after all, is what we try to do in the practice of frequent Confession. In what way, indeed, can frequent Confession and Holy Communion prove their efficacy and fruitfulness better than by producing a strong and healthy spirit of prayer in our lives? Frequent Confession, if well made, necessarily forms prayerful souls: Christian men and women who readily and frequently, indeed uninterruptedly, lift up their hearts to God and to Christ; who, in union with God and with Christ, live lives of continual adoration, praise, and thanksgiving, of petition and atonement. They fulfill the Savior's command that "we ought always to pray and not to faint" (Lk 18: 1).

This life of prayer is a distinguishing characteristic of the new supernatural man, the man who has been transformed by God's grace. He lives in an entirely different world from that of those who do not pray. The atmosphere of his life is not the same as that of those around him. His thoughts and aspirations and his whole soul are turned in quite another direction. He has not the same interests and aims as other men. When he undertakes something, his way of going about it is different from that of the man who does not pray. His outlook on the world and on life is clear and definite, but in many ways it is quite unlike that of others. The events and happenings of this world make less impression on him than on others, so much so that he is sometimes taken to be indifferent, cold, and apathetic. A serene and assured peace distinguishes him from those others whose entire energy is devoted to the struggle for worldly success and advancement.

2. In what does a life of prayer, continual prayer, consist? Not in an endless number of vocal prayers, not in uninterrupted interior prayer, not in thinking un-

ceasingly about God and the things of God, not in the soul's continual attention to God present in us and all about us. It does not consist in a certain number of acts, practices, aspirations, or ejaculations. It consists rather in a permanent attitude and direction of the will, as a result of which all that we do and suffer becomes one continual prayer.

Continual prayer consists in a steadfast disposition of love toward God, of trust in him, of submission to his holy will in all things: a disposition that has become so customary that it is second nature to us. It means that we are firmly determined never deliberately to do anything that would displease God or displease Christ our Savior. It means that we desire to live in the fullest conformity with God's will, to please God and Christ our Savior in all things, never to refuse anything to God or Christ, to accept everything from God's hands just as he gives it—work, duty, sacrifice, suffering, the circumstances of our lives, arrangements of various kinds, pleasures and joys.

Continual prayer does not mean that we are always thinking of God—though it does mean that we do not consciously entertain useless thoughts, much less evil ones. It does not mean that we have to be continually making acts and aspirations or always formulating prayers with our lips. Our mind is on our work or on whatever duty we are doing. But our heart and our will are ever directed toward God, ever attentive to him, ever ready to do his will and to submit to his will in all things. Constant prayer means living in complete forgetfulness of self, with all our desires and affections directed toward God.

Prayer is indeed a disposition, an inclination of the will, a union of the will with God and with Christ; it is love, self-surrender, obedience, quiet endurance, a right intention, holy zeal. This disposition is nourished by daily meditation. It shows itself in all our behavior: in our thoughts and judgments, in our hatred of evil, in our concern for God's interests; in vocal prayer and in oft repeated ejaculatory prayers, which, like flames, naturally and spontaneously, burst forth from the glowing fire of the love of God that is deep down in our hearts.

3. Such continual prayer, such a deep interior disposition of prayer, such an inclination of the will, such a holy readiness and determination to be entirely united with God's will and to surrender ourselves wholly to him: this should be the fruit of frequent Confession.

Genuine prayer has the power to transform and sanctify us both interiorly and exteriorly. If our prayer does not make us daily more resigned to the will of God, more detached from our own will, more submissive and patient, more obedient and humble and more charitable, more tolerant and forgiving, more kindly and gracious toward others: then it is not true and genuine. Genuine prayer produces a sincere desire and readiness to refer everything in our lives—all its circumstances and events, its failures and sufferings and troubles—to God, to do and accept all with resignation to God's will and in union with the intentions and prayer of the most Sacred Heart of Jesus. Such prayer will be the precious fruit of frequent Confession, by means of which the soul becomes ever purer, freer, more united to God and more transformed into the likeness of Christ.

Lord, teach us to pray. Amen.

CHAPTER TWENTY-SIX

Frequent Holy Communion

*"I am the bread of life. . . . If any man eat of this
bread, he shall live forever. . . . Amen, amen I say
unto you, except you eat the flesh of the Son of man
and drink his blood, you shall not have life in you."*
—JOHN 6: 48–53

1. We seek life, true life, the life promised by Christ.
And we find it in Holy Communion. In the other sacraments of the New Testament, it is only the power that
goes forth from Christ that is operative; he is not personally present in them with his divinity and humanity,
with his soul and body. But it is different in the sacrament of the Eucharist, in Holy Communion. Here and
here alone he is present in person under the appear-
ance of a tiny peace of bread: he, the author and source
of all graces, of all supernatural life. And he is present
not only with his divinity but also with his humanity,
with his body and soul. For what purpose? To give himself as our food. "My flesh is meat indeed" (Jn 6: 55).

Food preserves life, strengthens it, restores our lost
energy, gives us joy and gratification. And partaking of
this supernatural food has similar effects. It preserves
our supernatural life. It gives us strength to resist the
various harmful influences and temptations that
threaten us and to be a match for the wiles of our enemy, the devil, in his campaign against our souls. It

gives vigor to our supernatural life: that supernatural life which we possess as soon as we are in the state of sanctifying grace but which must go on increasing until we have arrived at the fullness of the Christian life. Hence we need the spiritual nourishment of Holy Communion. It restores what we lose—in spiritual energy and charity and fervor and zeal—during the course of ordinary daily life, through the indulgence of our passions and through our daily sins and faults. Finally, Holy Communion gives us a spiritual and supernatural joy—an exalted peace of soul—that makes the struggle easier for us, increases our courage, and gives us the strength for those sacrifices that a life of genuine imitation of Christ demands.

Holy Communion is the sacrament of union. Communion means union, becoming one. In the reception of Holy Communion a wonderful supernatural union takes place between Christ our Lord, who gives himself to us here to be our food, and our soul. Christ deigns to unite himself to us in a most intimate way, taking possession of our soul and sanctifying it to its inmost depths. He wants to become, as it were, *one* heart and *one* soul with us. His spirit, with its light, enters into our spirit, illuminates it with the light of faith, and enables us to see the events of life in God's light. We recognize vividly the vanity and nothingness of everything that is not God and that is not for God or does not lead to God. We see that nothing is really great or important for us except God and eternity.

The strong, noble, holy will of Christ unites itself to our will and cures it of its weakness, inconstancy, and selfishness. He shares his divine strength with us, so that, full of courage, we can say with St. Paul: "I can do all things in him who strengthens me" (Phil 4: 13). The strength of Christ supports us. We know that in his strength we can do everything and make any sacrifice, just as God asks. The heart of Christ, that heart flowing with ardent love for his father and for men, filled with all virtue and holiness, unites itself with our heart and enkindles our heart with its own fire. We feel ourselves carried along by a mighty urge to virtue, and there forms in us a lasting and unchangeable determination to do and suffer everything for God and to refuse him nothing.

Thus it is that Holy Communion transforms us. Gradually under its influence our thoughts, our outlook, and our principles change. We take over and make our own the thoughts, the outlook, and the principles of Christ. Likewise, our inclinations and our desires are transformed. We begin to will and desire and long for all that Christ wills and desires. Our heart begins to free itself from its inordinate self-love, from its purely natural inclinations and attachments, and our love turns more and more to God. The spirit of Christ lives in us and works in us. With St. Paul we say: "I live, now not I: but Christ liveth in me" and through me (Gal 2: 20).

And so we experience the fulfillment of Christ's promise: "He that eateth my flesh and drinketh my blood abideth in me and I in him" (Jn 6: 56)—not in the sense that Christ with his humanity, with his body and soul, continually dwells within us as long as we keep in the state of grace; but, rather, in the sense that, as a result of our Eucharistic union with him in Holy Communion, there remains afterward a special bond between him, the God-man, and our soul.

The Spirit of Christ, the Holy Spirit, who lives in the soul of Christ, lives also in us and stamps on us the likeness of Christ, and this as a result of the very close union into which Christ has entered with us in Holy Communion. "Christ is in us through his Spirit, whom he imparts to us and through whom he so acts within us that any divine effect operated in our souls by the Holy Spirit must be said to be operated in us also by Christ. The sacrament of the Eucharist gives to us the very author of supernatural grace, from whom we are enabled to draw that spirit of charity which bids us live not our own life but the life of Christ, and whereby we love the Redeemer himself in all the members of his social body" (*Mystici Corporis*, nos. 76, 82).

2. On December 20, 1905, Pope St. Pius X issued his now famous decree on frequent Communion. In it he laid down the conditions necessary for the frequent and daily reception of Holy Communion.

The fundamental principle always holds: *Sanctum sanctis* (holy things are for those who are holy). Only if we prepare well for it will Holy Communion and, in particular, frequent Communion produce in us the results that it should. It is, alas, possible to receive Holy Communion and even daily Communion in such a way that it leads not to sanctity but to destruction.

For the frequent or even daily reception of Holy Communion the decree of St. Pius lays down two necessary conditions: (1) We must be in the state of sanctifying grace, that is to say, we must not be conscious of any mortal sin on our soul. (2) In receiving Holy Communion we must have a right and pious intention (*cum recta piaque mente*). "A right intention," says the decree, "consists in this: that one approaches the holy table not just through routine or out of vanity or from any merely human motives, but in order to please God, to become more closely united to him by charity and to find a remedy for our infirmities and defects in this divine medicament."

The decree goes on to say expressly that, while it is very desirable that frequent and daily communicants should be free from venial sins, at least from those that are fully deliberate, and from all affection to venial sin, nevertheless, it suffices if they are free from mortal sin and are resolved to avoid sin for the future. And it adds: "If they have this genuine resolve not to sin any more, then without doubt, as a result of frequent Holy Communion, they will gradually become free from venial sin and from attachment to it." And if this fails to happen, what then? Some theologians say that in this case, namely, where we are continually falling back into sin notwithstanding our frequent Communion, the lack of fruit is due to the fact that something is wanting in our intention in approaching this divine banquet.

The decree leaves the regulation of the frequency of Holy Communion to the prudent judgment of one's confessor. Finally, it stresses the necessity of an adequate preparation for and thanksgiving after Holy Communion.

3. Is it correct to regard frequent Confession as a practice that was a good substitute for frequent Holy Communion in the time before the decree of St. Pius X on frequent Communion but that today really has no place? This view, put forward by some not so long ago, is by no means to be accepted. Both practices, frequent Confession and frequent Holy Communion, are most important and have their place in our spiritual formation. Pope Pius XII spoke decisively in favor of "the pious practice of frequent Confession," presupposing at the same time the frequent reception of Holy Communion (*Mystici Corporis*, no. 87; cf. no. 83). How often, in his many allocutions and addresses, did he not exhort the faithful to the reception of Holy Communion!

Frequent Confession and frequent Holy Communion go together. They both have one and the same end in view: victory over all sin and evil and the attainment of the perfection of the Christian life in holy charity. The better we make our frequent Confessions, the more surely and completely shall we ensure that "our bad habits are uprooted, spiritual negligence and apathy are prevented, and our conscience is purified" (*Mystici Corporis*, no. 87). We shall, as the Holy Father says in the same place, "grow in Christian humility"; and to the humble God gives his grace. Frequent Confession, indeed, plays a very important role with regard to the frequent reception of Holy Communion. It ensures that we strive diligently to have that "right intention" which is required, with all that it involves, and thus it helps very greatly to make our frequent Holy Communion more fruitful. Certainly those who spoke disparagingly of frequent Confession were not acting according to the mind of Pius XII as expressed in the encyclical already quoted. "Those who are diminishing esteem for frequent Confession," he wrote, "are to know that the enterprise upon which they have embarked is alien to the Spirit of Christ and most detrimental to the Mystical Body of our Savior" (ibid.).

Let us by all means practice frequent and daily Communion. But if we do, let us not think that we can therefore do without frequent Confession on the ground that Holy Communion too has the power of forgiving sins. Certainly Holy Communion can cause our past venial sins to be blotted out by means of the act of charity its reception impels us to make. But if we want to attack our venial sins directly and strive to overcome them (as those who practice frequent Confession do), then frequent Confession is necessary to support and assist the effects of Holy Communion. Besides, frequent Confession itself contributes to the increase of grace and charity in the soul and thus leads us to the same goal as Holy Communion.

It is, alas, a fact that, for many, frequent Holy Communion does not produce the fruit it should and that many are found wanting with regard to the necessary "right intention." For all these there can scarcely be any better means of improving their manner of receiving Holy Communion and making it really fruitful than to confess frequently with earnestness to a zealous and sincere priest who will take an interest in them and help them.

So let us hold both these practices as sacred and let us regard them both as precious gifts from God: frequent Confession and frequent and daily Holy Communion.

> *Lord, I am not worthy that thou should enter under my roof. Say but the word and my soul shall be healed. Amen.*

Index

Christian perfection, 49, 50–
    51, 62–63, 70, 96, 131–36,
    219–20, 222–23, 253–54
Church, the, 25, 32, 34, 40,
    127
    compunction and, 187–88
    Confession and, 11–12, 15–
        16, 28, 39, 43, 47–48, 50–
        53
    faults of frailty and, 124
    fear of God and, 211
    indulgences and, 183, 184,
        185
    liturgy of, 222, 234
    penance and, 14, 196, 198–
        99
    satisfaction and, 200
    self-love and, 144
    self-righteousness and, 165–
        66
    use of the sacraments and, 7–
        8, 18–19
    the virtue of hope and, 220
clergy, 10, 39, 53
    See also priests; religious, the
Code of Canon Law, 19, 30, 39,
    40
commandments, 65, 227–28
Communion. See Holy
    Communion
community, 47–48
compassion, 235–36
complacency, 234–35, 241–42
compunction of heart, 75,
    186–95
concupiscence, 154, 170, 213
Conferences of Bishops, 15
Confession
    abuse of, 57
    aim of, 48, 50–52
    as cleansing sacrament, 11

decline in the use of, 7–8
First, 15–20, 30–31
the forgiveness of Jesus in, 8
individual, 25–26
methods of, 64–66
opposition to, 39
as a personal sacrament, 76
the Redemption and, 31–33
sacramental nature of, 49
spiritual direction and, 48–49
confession
    of grave sin, 20–21
    purpose of amendment and,
        63, 70, 72
    of sin, 46, 52, 54, 62, 176
    of sins repeatedly, 49–50
    validity of, 56–57
confessional, apostolate of the,
    26–27, 31
Confessions (St. Augustine), 96
confessors
    availability of, 29–30
    duties of, 49
    imperfections and, 143
    occasions of faults and, 64
    penance and, 79
    penitent and, 62, 82–85
    role of, 65–66
    self-righteousness and, 171
    spiritual direction and, 62,
        81, 150
    See also priests; religious, the
Confirmation, 209
Confiteor, 44
Congregation for Religious,
    14–15
conscience, 28, 76, 86–91
    acting against, 43
    compunction and, 190
    examination of, 46, 55, 60,
        66–72, 90, 194, 243–44

frequent reception of, 13, 25,
51, 127, 167, 176, 187,
249–55
grace and, 209, 232–33
prayer and, 246
preparation to receive, 17,
19, 151
Holy Mass, 8, 44, 176, 238
Holy Spirit, 8–9, 18, 19, 24, 53,
96, 168, 208, 226, 230,
251–52
hope, 34, 220–21, 227
humility, 9, 14, 53, 98, 147,
191, 211, 254

Imitation of Christ, 215, 226–
27
Immaculate Mother, 21
imperfections, 62, 137–43,
189, 218–24, 245–46
indifference, 138, 139
indulgences, 33, 51, 183, 184,
185
Innocent XII, 220
"integrity of confession," 30
interior life
charity and, 242–43
compunction and, 186, 190,
192–93
development of, 9–10, 40, 55,
57–58, 64–66, 209–10
examination of conscience
and, 66–69
frequent Holy Communion
and, 249–50
humility and, 98–99
imperfections and, 62–63,
140
masters of, 9
perfection of, 129–36, 219
self-righteousness and, 167

sin and, 45–46, 109, 116,
127–28
spiritual direction and, 80–
81, 83
tepidity and, 152–54
the young Christian and, 16,
91
intolerance, 165–66
invincible error, 88

James, St., 124
Jesus Christ, 21, 25, 32, 44, 47,
50, 60, 84, 101
as the Bridegroom of souls,
51–52
the call to conversion and, 8,
9–10, 28
compunction and, 194
conformity to, 17
death of, 20, 78, 202
forgiveness of, 26, 30, 31
friendship and, 101–3
historical, 217
law of, 166
love of, 58–59, 115, 230–37
love of one's neighbor and,
239–40
Peter's denial of, 173–76
prayer and, 248
the priest as representative of,
80
satisfaction and, 199–200
the Sermon on the Mount
and, 130
sin and, 22, 95, 98, 113
as Son of God, 106–7
soul yearning for, 181
Spirit of, 39, 251–52
strength of, 150, 151
will of, 250
John, St., 76, 109, 235

priests (*continued*)
  Confession and, 7, 13–14, 20, 49
  duty of, 26–27
  and the ministry of reconciliation, 32–33
  penance and, 198–200
  as recipients of Confession, 12
  as representative of Christ, 80
  as representative of God, 82
  as the representative of the Church, 47–48
  role as confessors, 27–28
  See also confessors; religious, the
prodigal son, 20–22, 105–6
providence, 9, 119
punishment, 76, 196–200, 213, 219
Purgatory, 98, 180, 182–83, 184, 196, 212
purification, 25, 43, 50–51, 55, 134, 181
purpose of amendment, 55–61, 63, 69, 70–71, 72, 142, 174, 175, 244
  See also contrition

Reconciliation. *See* Confession
Redemption, 31–33
reflection, 14, 89
religious, the
  Christian perfection and, 62–63, 135
  Confession and, 14–15, 39, 49, 100
  imperfection and, 139
  spiritual direction and, 49
  tepidity and, 157
  See also confessors; priests

"religious exercise," 202
religious life. *See* interior life
Resurrection, 24
Rite of Penance, 1973, 20

Sacerdotii nostri primordia (Paul VI), 28
sacramentals, 44
sacraments, 11, 12–13, 16, 44, 185, 191, 204
Sacred Congregation for the Clergy, 17
Sacred Congregation for the Doctrine of the Faith, 20
Sacred Congregation for the Sacraments and Divine Worship, 17
sacrifice, 22, 78
saints, the, 96, 124, 187–88, 200
salvation, 170, 218–19, 242
sanctification, 222–23, 248
sanctifying grace, 45, 47, 50, 96, 107, 111–12, 128, 204, 207, 208–9, 252
satisfaction, 76–79, 196–203
Second Vatican Council, 7, 12–13, 26–27
self, 14, 22, 145–46, 150
self-assurance, spiritual, 170–71
self-hatred, 145–146, 150
self-interested love, 218–24
self-knowledge, 9, 150, 171
self-love, 120, 126, 144–51, 222–23
self-righteousness, 165–72
seminarians, 49, 135
Sermon on the Mount, 129–31, 137
"simply servile fear," 214, 215

sin, 101–8
  absence of, 13
  accusation of, 46, 54, 62, 176
  actual, 30
  avoidance of, 137
  awareness of, 8, 28–29, 34,
    76
  compunction and, 186–90,
    192, 194
  conscience and, 90
  contrition and, 72, 74–75,
    174
  deliberate, 51
  effect of, 20–21, 182–83,
    201–2, 205–6
  faults of frailty and, 123–24
  fear of God and, 212–15,
    216–7
  of frailty, 55–58, 62, 67, 97,
    122–28, 183, 189
  freedom from, 228–29
  grace and, 50
  grave, 21
  imperfections and, 139–40,
    142
  interior aversion of heart
    from, 45
  of malice, 122
  nature of, 15, 30
  of omission, 76, 158–64
  penance and, 96–97, 98, 99,
    179
  repeated confession of, 49–
    50
  satisfaction for, 196–203
  self-love and, 145
  self-righteousness and, 166
  structure of, 34–35
  See also mortal sin; venial sin
"slavishly servile fear," 213
sloth, 214

sorrow. See compunction of the
    heart
soul, 66, 152, 154
  cleansing of, 44
  confession and the, 45–46
  examination of conscience
    and, 66–67
  God and, 134, 189
  love and, 120
  perfection of, 51–52
  purification of, 43, 50–51, 55
  sin and, 111–12, 174, 229
  sorrow of the, 186–95
  usefulness of Confession for
    the, 48
spiritual direction, 14–15, 48–
    49, 81–82, 150
spirituality, 9, 85, 192
spiritual life. See interior life
suffering, 78, 200–3
Summa theologica (Thomas
    Aquinas), 74
supernatural life. See interior
    life
Synod of Bishops, 1983, 33–34

Ten Commandments, 91
tenet of Molinos, 67
tepidity, 9, 51, 63, 108, 152–
    57
Teresa of Avila, St., 189
Thomas Aquinas, St., 74, 78
timor filialis Dei, 214, 216
timor serviliter servilis, 213
timor simpliciter servilis, 214, 215

venial sin, 30
  belittling of, 12
  Christian perfection and, 135
  compunction and, 189, 193–
    94